Quod scriptura, non iubet vetat

The Latin translates, "What is not commanded in scripture, is forbidden:'

On the Cover: Baptists rejoice to hold in common with other evangelicals the main principles of the orthodox Christian faith. However, there are points of difference and these differences are significant. In fact, because these differences arise out of God's revealed will, they are of vital importance. Hence, the barriers of separation between Baptists and others can hardly be considered a trifling matter. To suppose that Baptists are kept apart solely by their views on Baptism or the Lord's Supper is a regrettable misunderstanding. Baptists hold views which distinguish them from Catholics, Congregationalists, Episcopalians, Lutherans, Methodists, Pentecostals, and Presbyterians, and the differences are so great as not only to justify, but to demand, the separate denominational existence of Baptists. Some people think Baptists ought not teach and emphasize their differences but as E.J. Forrester stated in 1893, "Any denomination that has views which justify its separate existence, is bound to promulgate those views. If those views are of sufficient importance to justify a separate existence, they are important enough to create a duty for their promulgation ... the very same reasons which justify the separate existence of any denomination make it the duty of that denomination to teach the distinctive doctrines upon which its separate existence rests." If Baptists have a right to a separate denominational life, it is their duty to propagate their distinctive principles, without which their separate life cannot be justified or maintained.

Many among today's professing Baptists have an agenda to revise the Baptist distinctives and redefine what it means to be a Baptist. Others don't understand why it even matters. The books being reproduced in the *Baptist Distinctives Series* are republished in order that Baptists from the past may state, explain and defend the primary Baptist distinctives as they understood them. It is hoped that this Series will provide a more thorough historical perspective on what it means to be distinctively Baptist.

The Lord Jesus Christ asked, *"And why call ye me, Lord, Lord, and do not the things which I say?"* (Luke 6:46). The immediate context surrounding this question explains what it means to be a true disciple of Christ. Addressing the same issue, Christ's question is meant to show that a confession of discipleship to the Lord Jesus Christ is inconsistent and untrue if it is not accompanied with a corresponding submission to His authoritative commands. Christ's question teaches us that a true recognition of His authority as Lord inevitably includes a submission to the authority of His Word. Hence, with this question Christ has made it forever impossible to separate His authority as King from the authority of His Word. These two principles—the authority of Christ as King and the authority of His Word—are the two most fundamental Baptist distinctives. The first gives rise to the second and out of these two all the other Baptist distinctives emanate. As F.M. Iams wrote in 1894, "Loyalty to Christ as King, manifesting itself in a constant and unswerving obedience to His will as revealed in His written Word, is the real source of all the Baptist distinctives:' In the search for the *primary* Baptist distinctive many have settled on the Lordship of Christ as the most basic distinctive. Strangely, in doing this, some have attempted to separate Christ's Lordship from the authority of Scripture, as if you could embrace Christ's authority without submitting to what He commanded. However, while Christ's Lordship and Kingly authority can be isolated and considered essentially for discussion's sake, we see from Christ's own words in Luke 6:46 that His Lordship is really inseparable from His Word and, with regard to real Christian discipleship, there can be no practical submission to the one without a practical submission to the other.

In the symbol above the Kingly Crown and the Open Bible represent the inseparable truths of Christ's Kingly and Biblical authority. The Crown and Bible graphics are supplemented by three Bible verses (Ecclesiastes 8:4, Matthew 28:18-20, and Luke 6:46) that reiterate and reinforce the inextricable connection between the authority of Christ as King and the authority of His Word. The truths symbolized by these components are further emphasized by the Latin quotation - *quod scriptura, non iubet vetat*— i.e., "What is not commanded in scripture, is forbidden:' This Latin quote has been considered historically as a summary statement of the regulative principle of Scripture. Together these various symbolic components converge to exhibit the two most foundational Baptist Distinctives out of which all the other Baptist Distinctives arise. Consequently, we have chosen this composite symbol as a logo to represent the primary truths set forth in the *Baptist Distinctives Series*.

"Close Communion:"

or, baptism as a prerequisite to the lord's supper

JOHN T. CHRISTIAN
1854-1925

"CLOSE COMMUNION:"

OR, BAPTISM AS A PREREQUISITE TO THE LORD'S SUPPER.

BY

JOHN T. CHRISTIAN, A.M., D.D.,

Author of "Immersion, the Act of Christian Baptism," etc.

With a Biographical Sketch of the Author by John Franklin Jones

---

SECOND EDITION.

LOUISVILLE, KY.
BAPTIST BOOK CONCERN.
1892.

he Baptist Standard Bearer, Inc.
NUMBER ONE IRON OAKS DRIVE • PARIS, ARKANSAS 72855

Thou hast given a *standard* to them that fear thee;
that it may be displayed because of the truth.
− *Psalm 60:4*

Reprinted 2006

by

THE BAPTIST STANDARD BEARER, INC.
No. 1 Iron Oaks Drive
Paris, Arkansas 72855
(479) 963-3831

THE WALDENSIAN EMBLEM
lux lucet in tenebris
"The Light Shineth in the Darkness"

ISBN# 1579784143

PREFACE.

THE position of the Baptists upon the Communion question is one of neutrality. We do not invite others to participate with us; and not inviting others we do not accept invitations. Our position is defensive rather than offensive. This book is written in this spirit. It is intended to explain and defend the practice commonly known as "Close Communion."

We think our practice is Scriptural. The brotherhood of the New Testament were one in fellowship and doctrines. Under those conditions open communion was impossible. This view is confirmed by all history. I have been unable to find an instance of open communion for the first sixteen hundred years after Christ.

I am in no way responsible for the opinions of the authors I quote, only so far as I may endorse them. Many of these writers believe in baptismal salvation, in baptism coming in the room of circumcision, and other errors which we repudiate. I have, however, accurately examined original sources, so that there may be no doubt as to the testimony of these writers.

The author desires that this book may be read in the kind spirit in which it was written. There are many hard facts in the book, but no hard words. I merely recorded facts as I found them without passion or prejudice.

CONTENTS.

PAGE

CHAPTER I.
Are Ignorance, Prejudice, and Bigotry the Reasons Why Baptists are Close Communionists? 7

CHAPTER II.
The Baptist Position Stated and Defended by the Scriptures 21

CHAPTER III.
The Testimony of the Fathers 39

CHAPTER IV.
The Testimony of Scholars........................... 50

CHAPTER V.
The Testimony of Creeds, Confessions, etc............ 61

CHAPTER VI.
The Terms of Communion in the Episcopal Church. Are the Episcopalians Close Communionists?..... 64

CHAPTER VII.
The Terms of Communion in the Presbyterian Church. Are the Presbyterians Close Communionists?..... 81

CHAPTER VIII.
The Terms of Communion in the Congregational Church. Are the Congregationalists Close Communionists?......................................109

CHAPTER IX.
The Terms of Communion in the Methodist Church. Are the Methodists Close Communionists? The Wesleys and Dr. Coke............................118

CONTENTS.

CHAPTER X.
The Terms of Communion in the Methodist Church. Are the Methodists Close Communionists? Asbury and Hedding. The Discipline. Living Bishops. Watson and Others.................................138

CHAPTER XI.
The Terms of Communion of the Disciples or Christian Church. Are the Disciples Close Communionists? 156

CHAPTER XII.
What Is Baptism?.....................................163

CHAPTER XIII.
Are Baptists Lacking in Charity?.....................190

CHAPTER XIV.
Positive and Moral Law...............................197

CHAPTER XV.
Open Communion Destroys Gospel Discipline.........202

CHAPTER XVI.
Infant Communion....................................212

CHAPTER XVII.
Open Communionists Do Not Endorse Each Other....220

CHAPTER XVIII.
Open Communion is a Worn Out Heresy Borrowed From the Baptists.................................234

"CLOSE COMMUNION;"

OR, BAPTISM AS A PREREQUISITE TO THE LORD'S SUPPER.

CHAPTER I.

ARE IGNORANCE, PREJUDICE, AND BIGOTRY THE REASONS WHY BAPTISTS ARE CLOSE COMMUNIONISTS?

THE Baptists have been thoroughly misunderstood on the subject of Close Communion; and it has been difficult to get our real opinions before the world. That we are more illiberal, un-Christian, and sectarian than others I do not believe. Perhaps it is frequently more convenient and popular to use denunciatory words than to meet our arguments. Our position has been distorted, and some of those professing the broadest liberality have sometimes called us the harshest names. I shall notice a few of these epithets not for the purpose of stirring up ill feeling and strife, for of that there has been too much already, but rather that we may have the subject fairly before our minds. I believe that we can easily show that these names have no more application to us than to others.

We have been called "bigoted." Webster says that in its origin the word bigot means "hypocrite," and defines it: "One obstinately and unreasonably wedded to a particular religious creed, opinion, practice or ritual." Hypocrites we are not. It is proverbial that the Baptists are among the boldest and most progressive people on earth; and that they have been swift, in all proper ways, to promulgate their opinions. To the charge of being obstinately and unreasonably wedded to an opinion we plead not guilty. And as to creed or ritual it is not so much as mentioned among us. The fact that our doctrines and practices do not agree with what others believe on those subjects, does not, in the least, go to prove that we are not grounded upon the truth. Our highest appeal is not to the bar of public opinion, but to the Word of God. We stand by the Bible. When God commands a thing, we believe men ought to obey. When men object to this position we make answer: "Whether it be right in the sight of God to hearken unto you more than unto God, judge ye." (Acts 4:19.) If this is not popular with so-called liberal opinions, as it is not, we can only say: "We ought to obey God rather than men." (Acts 5:29.) We must have a "thus saith the Lord." We should not be criticised because we refuse to obey the commandments of men.

Many wholly mistake latitudinarianism for

catholicism. I do not think John Wesley ever said a truer thing than what he says on this point. Said he: "A catholic spirit is not speculative latitudinarianism. It is not an indifference to all opinions. This is the spawn of hell; not the offspring of heaven. This unsettledness of thought, this being driven to and fro, and tossed about by every wind of doctrine, is a great curse, not a blessing; an irreconcilable enemy, not a true catholicism. A man of a true catholic spirit does not halt between two opinions; nor vainly endeavor to blend them into one. Observe this, you that know not what spirit you are of; who call yourself a catholic spirit, only because you are of a muddy understanding; because your mind is all in a mist; because you are of no settled, consistent principles, but are for jumbling all opinions together. Be convinced that you have quite missed your way. You know not where you are. You think you have got into the very Spirit of Christ; when in truth you are nearer the spirit of Anti-Christ." (Rowland Hill's Full Answer to J. Wesley's Remarks, pp. 40, 41.)

It ought to be popular for a man to have convictions and stand by them. For my part I like a man who believes something and knows why he believes it; and when occasion calls for it is not afraid to defend his position. "The appointment of God," says Turretin, "is the highest law, the supreme necessity; which we ought rather to obey than indulge popular ignorance and weakness." (Inst. Theol., Tom. iii, Loc. xix, Quaes. xiv, sec. 14, p. 336.) This is the height and front of our offending. We recognize no man as Lord of the conscience. I, therefore, appeal from the position that we are hypocrites and obstinate.

CHRISTIAN UNION.

The Baptists of the United States stand publicly pledged to unite at any time with any or all Christian denominations, upon the Word of God. We are in favor of Christian union, not upon "the historic episcopacy," or upon historic anything else, but upon the Bible. There is nothing unreasonable in this demand. If it is bigotry to say that God's Word is right, then we plead guilty. In another place I will show the evil results of Open Communion upon Christian charity; but here I plead only that we are not uncharitable and illiberal. The Southern Baptist Convention and the Northern Anniversaries unanimously passed the following resolutions:

"WHEREAS, The different denominations have lately been giving unusual attention to the subject of Christian union, and

"WHEREAS, It is conceded to be a great desideratum that Christians should agree in all important points of doctrine and polity, and

"WHEREAS, There is a standard recognized as

authoritative by all Christians, viz: the Bible, therefore,

"*Resolved*, By the Southern Baptist Convention (and the same resolutions were passed by the Northern Anniversaries), representing 1,200,000 communicants, that we recognize the gravity of the problem of bringing different denominations to see alike on important subjects concerning which they now differ, and they recognize in the teaching of Scripture the only basis on which such an agreement is either possible or desirable, also

"*Resolved*, That we respectfully propose to the general bodies of our brethren of other denominations to select representative scholars who shall consider and seek to determine just what is the teaching of the Bible on the leading points of difference of doctrine and polity between the denominations, in the hope that they can at least help to a better understanding of the issues involved; also

"*Resolved*, That we heartily favor that the results of the proposed conference of representative scholars be widely published in all denominational papers so that the Christian public can be thoroughly informed concerning these results, and that progress may be made toward true Christian union."

As long as this invitation remains unaccepted no one has a right to declare that we are uncharitable and illiberal. This can not be true: for we are not only in favor of toleration, but of the widest liberty in all matters of conscience. We believe that the civil law has nothing to do with religion; and that it is a heaven-given privilege for every man to worship according to the dictates of his own conscience. We must stand or fall before God; and man is not our judge. All we ask is that we shall have the same right to worship God that we cheerfully grant to others. We have been pioneers in this work. "Freedom of conscience," says Mr. Bancroft, the brilliant historian of the United States, "unlimited freedom of mind, was, from the first, the trophy of the Baptists."

For the wonderful change that has taken place in England, Dr. Schaff gives the credit to the Baptists. "For this change of public sentiment," says he, "the chief merit is due to the English Non-conformists, who in the school of persecution became advocates of toleration, especially to the Baptists and Quakers, who made religious liberty (within the limits of the golden rule) an article of their creed so that they could not consistently persecute even if they should ever have a chance to do so." (Creeds of Christ., vol. 1, p. 803.)

The historian, Skeats, who was not a Baptist, records these strong words: "It is the singular and the distinguished honor of the Baptists to have repudiated, from their earliest history, all coercive power over the consciences and actions of men with reference to religion. No sentence is to be found in all of their writings inconsistent with these principles of Christian liberty and willinghood which are now equally dear to all of the free Congregational churches of England. They were the photo-evangelists of the voluntary principle." (History of the Free Churches of England, p. 24.)

So strikingly correct and sympathetic are the words of Gervinus, the most astute and philosophic of the German historians of this century, that I present them here. He says: "In accordance with these principles Roger Williams insisted, in Massachusetts, upon allowing entire freedom of conscience, and upon the entire separation of the Church and the State. But he was obliged to flee, and in 1636 he formed in Rhode Island a small and new society, in which perfect freedom in matters of faith was allowed, and in which the majority ruled in all civil affairs. Here in a little State, the fundamental principles of political and ecclesiastical liberty practically prevailed, before they were ever taught in any of the schools of philosophy in Europe. At that time people predicted only a short existence of these democratical experiments: universal suffrage, universal eligibility to office, the annual change of rulers, perfect religious freedom—

the Miltonian doctrines of schisms. But not only have these ideas and these forms of government maintained themselves here, but precisely from this little State have they extended themselves throughout the United States. They have conquered the aristocratic tendencies in Carolina and New York, the High Church in Virginia, the Theocracy in Massachusetts, and the monarchy in all America. They have given laws to a continent, and formidable through their moral influence, they lie at the bottom of all the democratic movements which are now shaking the nations of Europe."

I shall venture to quote the complimentary letter of George Washington to the Baptists. He says: "I have often expressed my sentiments that every man conducting himself as a good citizen, and being accountable alone to God for his religious opinions, ought to be protected in worshipping according to the dictates of his own conscience, while I recollect, with satisfaction, that the religious society of which you are members have been throughout America, uniformly and almost unanimously the firm friends of civil liberty, and the preserving promoters of our glorious revolution, I can not hesitate to believe that they will be faithful supporters of a free, yet efficient, general government. Under this pleasing expectation, I rejoice to assure them that they may rely on my best wishes and endeavors to advance their prosperity."

I can not believe that people who thus love liberty, and contend for the widest freedom of thought and worship, will be either uncharitable or illiberal. We must look for some other reason for Close Communion.

The last cry is that the Baptists are ignorant. We freely confess that we have among us more ignorance than has ever done us any good. But the denomination that can not reach the ignorant and the poor lacks one of the essential features of a church of Christ. There are those, however, who appear honestly to believe that we hold to Close Communion through sheer ignorance. While it is a fact that among our millions we have many unlettered people, it is equally a fact that in scholarly attainments and educational facilities we occupy no mean place. I quote the tribute of the great Presbyterian, Dr. Chalmers, to the English Baptists. He evidently thought they had done something for the world. He says: "Let it never be forgotten of the Particular Baptists of England, that they form the denomination of Fuller and Carey and Ryland and Hall and Foster; that they have organized among the greatest of all missionary enterprises; that they have enriched the Christian literature of our country with authorship of the most exalted piety, as well as with the first talent, and the first eloquence; that they have waged a very noble and successful war with the hydra of Antinomianism; that perhaps there is not a more intellectual community of ministers in our islands, or who have put forth to their number a greater amount of mental power and mental activity in the defence and illustration of our common faith; and, what is better than all of the triumphs of genius or understanding, who by their zeal and fidelity and pastoral labor among congregations which they have reared, have done more to swell the list of genuine discipleship in the walks of private society—and thus to both uphold and extend the living Christianity of our nation." (Com. Romans, Lec. 14, p. 76.)

In the United States the Baptists are in the front rank in providing educational facilities. Our ministers in scholarly ability are second to none; and our schools are of the very best. We have always been the advocates of education. The oldest and largest University in the United States is Harvard. The first money it ever received for an endowment was from a Baptist; and the Hollis family—Baptists—were among its most munificent benefactors. Its first two Presidents, Henry Dunster and Charles Chausey, were Baptists. President Quincey said of them: "For learning and talents they have been surpassed by no one of their successors." The Baptists assisted Franklin in laying the foundations of the University of Pennsylvania, and have been among the first in their support of all State

IGNORANCE AND PREJUDICE. 17

schools. As early a 1764, when numbering in all America only 60 churches and about 5,000 members, the Baptists founded their first college, Brown University of Rhode Island. Now they have 28 chartered colleges, over 200 academies and female colleges, and 9 theological seminaries. In less than five years they have founded a university in Chicago, upon a wider plane than any school in America, with an endowment already little less than four millions of dollars. Nearly all of our colleges have recently added largely to their endowment funds. We have one man, Mr. J. D. Rockefeller, who has given nearly three millions of dollars for education.

The Baptists have 70 newspapers in the United States and not a few quarterlies and reviews.

In writers they have been second to none. The book that has reached a wider circulation than any other except the Bible, and has been translated into every tongue of earth, was written by a Baptist, John Bunyan. John Milton, author of Paradise Lost, was a Baptist. Macaulay calls these two the original minds of their century. Gill has not been surpassed as a commentator; and indeed time would fail us to speak of the multitude that we could mention with propriety.

All this and more has been frankly conceded by others.

Dr. Baird, in his great work, Religion in

America, p. 463, says: "The ministry of the Baptists comprehends a body of men who, in point of talent, learning and eloquence, as well as devoted piety, have no superiors in this country."

Dr. T. L. Cuyler recently said of the Baptists in Philadelphia and elsewhere: "They are a powerful body in Philadelphia. Let us thank God that their great army corps all over the land are so stoutly loyal to sound doctrine and evangelical doctrine and progress."

The late Dr. Woods, of Andover, thus expressed himself: "I entertain the most cordial esteem, love and confidence toward the Baptists as a denomination. I have the freest intercourse, and the sincerest friendship with Baptist ministers, theological students, and private Christians. I have wished that our denomination—the Congregationalist—was as free from erratic speculations, and as well grounded in the doctrines and experimental principles of the Puritans as the Baptists. It seems to me that they are the Christians who are likely to maintain pure Christianity, and to hold fast the form of sound words."

Dr. Hase, the German historian, says: "They agree with, and even exceed the Congregationalists in their rejection of all human authority in matters of faith, and in their practical maintenance of the independence of the congregation." (Hist. of Christ. Ch., p. 603.)

The Baptists have taken the lead in modern

times in the cause of Foreign Missions and in the founding of Bible societies. In 1792, under Carey, they formed the first missionary society of modern times to preach the gospel to the heathen. When Carey made the proposition to send the gospel to India Dr. Ryland was so astounded at its audacity that he sprang to his feet and ordered Carey to sit down, saying: "When God pleases to convert the heathen, he will do it without your aid or mine." But the Baptist cobbler became the forerunner of the mighty mission work of to-day.

The Rev. J. L. Withrow recently said: "The Baptist church is in repute for thorough-going piety; a piety which takes the Bible as God's book, rather than as a book with some stray breaths of God through it, no one being sure where to find them; a piety which grasps the doctrines of justifying and sanctifying and glorifying grace with a grip which holds as a vice; a piety which one hundred years ago, before any other Protestant soul or society began it, arose to the divinest enterprises of Christianity, the enterprises of sending the gospel to all the ends of the earth. It was Baptist piety which did that. It was Baptist believers who began that monthly concert of prayer for Foreign Missions which has been heaping up prayers before the throne of God for a century, and adding to them every month petitions by the million! What a church it is to the glory of the Son of God and the good of this needy world!"

As an outgrowth of this mission work, in 1804, the British and Foreign Bible Society was formed. Joseph Hughes, a Baptist minister, bore the most prominent part in its organization. As one has quaintly put it: "He was the hands and feet, as he had been the head of the institution."

I think with all of these facts before me, that none of these are the reasons that Baptists have for believing in, and practicing, Close Communion. It is not held by them on account of ignorance, bigotry or selfishness. It may be that their practice is founded upon the Scriptures.

CHAPTER II.

THE BAPTIST POSITION STATED AND DEFENDED BY THE SCRIPTURES.

THE Baptists are strict communionists and are likely to remain such. We want to be just as close as the Word of God. If we have prospered as a people, it is because we have rigidly adhered to the Word of God. Whenever we turn aside from this well-trodden path for mere sentimentality or transient popularity, the day of our power and usefulness is gone. We are compelled to search for the old paths, and when we have found them to walk in them. Despite all criticisms and abuse we have prospered as strict communionists. The reason is not far away. In the face of all clamor we have adhered to God's Word and God has greatly honored us. What he has done in the past he will do in the future. There is neither argument nor wisdom in open communion. It is based upon mere sentiment, and that a false sentiment. We are strict communionists and we are going to remain strict.

This is freely admitted by Rev. J. L. Withrow, Presbyterian, in an able article in the *Interior*.

He says: "Furthermore, in their favor it is to be said, they have proved, beyond peradventure, that narrow church doors and severe communion conditions do not bar people out of the Christian church. Against creeds and communion bars there is ceaseless outcry from some quarters. The Baptists have no chaptered creed, but their unwritten creed, as England's unwritten constitution, is more insurmountable than the Thirty-nine Articles of Episcopacy, or the ponderous chapters of the Westminster Confession. Against chaptered creeds the complaints are so urgent that Congregationalists have recently made a new one—you may safely offer a dollar for every new convert which has been captured by that new creed who otherwise would not have been secured. And now the Presbyterians are wasting a heap of hard-earned money (contributed, much of it, by God's poor for better purposes), and are stirring bad blood between the brethren in an attempt to smooth off and sweeten up their creed. The claim is that we keep people out of the church, and candidates out of our ministry with such strict conditions as now exist. It sounds like arrant nonsense in presence of the fact that the Baptist church is the strictest church we have; and yet it is growing—not as a weed, but as the Word of God is promised to grow. There is no church, so far as we know, into which it is more difficult to enter than the

Baptist through theological, ecclesiastical and ceremonial conditions. And yet there are throngs pressing through its narrow threshold. Whoever cares to study this subject of easy and exacting conditions of church membership, asking which is most likely to secure accessions to the fellowship of professing Christians, should compare the history of the Baptist church with that of the liberal churches, so-called."

The practice of restricted communion is no arbitrary affair with us. We think the Lord has laid down in the New Testament certain

PREREQUISITES TO THE COMMUNION.

We think the Scriptures warrant definite terms of approach to the Lord's Supper. The divine order is, first, faith; second, baptism; third, church membership; fourth, discipline; fifth, doctrine; sixth, the Lord's Supper. No man has a right to the Lord's table who has not exercised faith, been baptized, and is a member of the church, subject to its discipline, and agreeing with it in doctrine. This is so important that I shall illustrate and defend it from a number of standpoints.

The Lord Jesus himself instituted the Supper. A record of this event is given in Matthew 26:26–30: "And as they were eating, Jesus took bread, and blessed it, and brake it, and gave it to the disciples, and said, Take, eat; this is my body. And he took the cup, and gave thanks, and gave it to them, saying, Drink ye all of it; for this is my blood of the new testament, which is shed for many for the remission of sins. But I say unto you, I will not drink henceforth of this fruit of the vine, until that day when I drink it new with you in my Father's kingdom. And when they had sung a hymn, they went out into the mount of Olives."

We have no right to change a qualification. Were these disciples baptized? There is no doubt about it. Robert Hall, the foremost defender of open communion, admits this. He says: "It is almost certain that some, probably the most of them, had been baptized by John." (Works, vol. 1, p. 303.) In the Gospel of John at least four of the disciples were declared to be disciples of John the Baptist. (1:36–40.) Jesus also made and baptized disciples. (John 4:1.) It is not reasonable to suppose that Jesus would have selected men to represent himself, who had refused to obey the first and plainest command of the Gospel. "The practice of the first Christian church," says Knapp, "confirms the point that the baptism of John was considered essentially the same with Christian baptism. For those who acknowledged that they had professed, by the baptism of John, to believe in Jesus as the Christ, and who in consequence of this had become in fact his disciples, and had believed in him, were not, in a single instance, baptized again into Christ, because this was considered as having been already done. Hence we do not find that any apostle or any other disciple of Jesus was the second time baptized; not even that Apollos mentioned in Acts xviii:25, because he had before believed in Jesus Christ, although he had received only the baptism of John." (Christ. Theol., p. 485.)

But the Scriptures do not leave us in doubt on this subject. When an apostle was to be chosen in the place of Judas Iscariot, he was required to be a disciple of John, as were the rest of the apostles. I quote Acts 1:21,22: "Wherefore of those men which have accompanied with us all the time that the Lord Jesus went in and out among us, *beginning from the baptism of John*, unto that same day that he was taken up from us, must one be ordained to be a witness with us of his resurrection."

This passage undoubtedly teaches that an apostle must have been a disciple of John. In fact this is made an absolute qualification. This interpretation is sustained by the foremost scholars.

Alexander, Presbyterian, says: "The idea evidently is, that the candidate must not only have believed Christ's doctrines and submitted to his teaching, as a disciple in the widest sense, but formed a part of that more permanent body, which appears to have attended him from place to place, throughout the whole course of his public ministry." (Acts of the Apostles Expl.)

Gloag says: "In these verses Peter assigns the necessary qualifications of the new apostle. He must have associated with them during all of the time that the Lord Jesus went in and out among them; that is, during the whole of his public ministry. He states the commencement of that period to be the baptism of John, and its termination to be the day of the ascension." (Crit. and Exeget. Com. on Acts.)

Burkitt says: "That is one who had followed Christ from his baptism to his ascension."

Adam Clarke, Methodist, says: "They judged it necessary to fill up this blank in the apostolate, by a person who had been an *eye witness* of the acts of our Lord. *Went in and out.* A phrase which includes all the actions of life. Beginning from the baptism of John. From the time that Christ was baptized by John in Jordan; for it was at that time that his public ministry properly began." (Com., vol. 3, p. 694.)

Barnes, Presbyterian, says: "The word 'beginning from' in the original refers to the Lord Jesus. The meaning may be thus expressed, 'during the time in which the Lord Jesus, beginning (his ministry) at the time he was baptized by John, went in and out among us, until the time in which he was taken up,' etc. From those who had during that time been the constant companions of the Lord Jesus must one be taken, who would thus be a witness of his whole ministry."

It is no answer to assert that John's baptism was not Christian baptism; for beyond doubt this was all the baptism Christ ever received, and none of the persons baptized by John were ever rebaptized. It answers every requirement of the Lord Jesus and we ought to be satisfied. "The object of John's baptism," says Knapp, "was the same of that of Christian; and from this it may be at once concluded that it did not differ essentially from the latter. John exhorted the persons baptized by him to repentance and to faith in the Messiah who was shortly to appear, and make these duties obligatory upon them by this rite. And as soon as Jesus publicly appeared, John asserted in the most forcible manner that he was the Messiah, and so required of all whom he had then or before baptized, that they should believe in Jesus as the Messiah. Now in Christian baptism, repentance and faith in Jesus as the Messiah are likewise the principal things which are required on the part of the subjects of this rite." (Christ. Theol., p. 485.)

Turrettin maintains with great learning and force that "the baptism of John was the same essentially with that of Christ," or Christian baptism.

Calvin says: "This makes it perfectly certain that the ministry of John was the very same as that which was afterwards delegated to the apostles. For the different hands by which baptism is administered do not make it a different baptism, but sameness of doctrine proves it to be the same. John and the apostles agreed in one doctrine. Both baptized unto repentance, both for the remission of sins, both in the name of Christ, from whom repentance and remission of sins proceed. John pointed to him as the Lamb of God who taketh away the sin of the world, thus describing him as the victim accepted of the Father, the propitiation of righteousness, and the author of salvation. What could the apostles add to this confession?" (Inst. Christ. Relig., vol. 3, pp. 332, 333.)

We are not, therefore, left in doubt about baptism preceding the Lord's Supper.

You will also notice that in the celebration of this first Supper there was no one present except the twelve apostles. His mother was not there; Mary, Martha and Lazarus were not present; the seventy were not admitted, indeed there were no other participants, and no spectators. There was no foolish sentimentality about this observance. Not one argument that open communionists urge can be based upon the institution of the Supper by Jesus.

This is the teaching of the great commission.

THE BAPTIST POSITION STATED. 29

Matthew 28:19,20, states: "Go, ye therefore, and teach all nations, baptizing them into the name of the Father, and of the Son, and of the Holy Ghost; teaching them to observe all things whatsoever I have commanded you: and, lo, I am with you alway, even unto the end of the world." I love to go back to foundation principles, and learn what Christ has commanded, and then I know how to obey. By this law we are required in the first place, to teach or preach the Gospel; secondly, to baptize those who believe; and thirdly, to instruct such baptized believers to observe all things whatsoever Christ has commanded; and the order in which these several duties are here stated, is as imperative as the duties themselves.

This argument is so important, and the logic of Dr. Hibbard, the Methodist writer, so just, that I transcribe a paragraph from him. "The reader will perceive," says he, "that the argument is based entirely upon the ORDER of the apostolic commission. It may be questioned by some whether the argument is genuine, and whether it is entitled to any considerable force. But suppose we assume an opposite ground? Suppose we say that the *things* commanded are important to be done, but the *order* observed in the commission is a subject of indifference. Now what will be the consequences of this position? What but total and irretrievable confusion? The apostles go forth; they are intent upon doing *all* that Christ commanded them, but the order of the duties is a subject of indifference. The consequence is that some are baptized before they are converted from heathenism; some receive the holy supper before either baptism or conversion; others are engaged in a course of instruction before they are discipled; and the most incoherent and unsuitable practices everywhere prevail. Improper persons are baptized, or baptism is improperly delayed; the holy supper is approached before the candidate is duly prepared, and it is therefore desecrated, or it is unduly withheld from rightful communicants. Is not the prescribed ORDER, therefore, in the administration of the ordinances, and the duties of the apostolic commission, all important? And thus we hold that Christ *enjoined* the *order* as well as the *duties* themselves; and, in this order of Christ, baptism precedes communion at the Lord's table." (Hibbard on Bapt., P. 2, p. 177.)

The custom of the apostles is in line with the commands of Christ. The divine order is beautifully set forth in Acts 2:41,42: "Then they that gladly received the word were baptized: and the same day there were added unto them three thousand souls. And they continued steadfastly in the apostle's doctrine and fellowship, and in breaking of bread and in prayers." The order is, teaching, gladly receiving the word, baptism, and the Lord's Supper. The Syriac, the oldest existing translation of the New Testament so understands this passage.

Calvin says: "I would have breaking of bread understood of the Lord's Supper." (Com. on Acts.)

Blount, Episcopalian, says: "I consider 'the fellowship' or 'communion' and 'the breaking of bread' to stand in close combination, and to indicate that another bond by which these first Christians were joined to the apostles, to one another, and to a unity in Christ, was a collective participation in the Lord's Supper." (Christ. Ch. First Three Cent.)

Baumgarten, Presbyterian, says: "The third characteristic that is noticed in respect to the baptized is the breaking of bread. The communion of the Lord with his disciples may very properly be characteristic that the disciples who, after his resurrection, had recognized him neither by his form nor by his discourse, immediately knew him upon his breaking of bread with them. This mode of communion was thereby consecrated; and appears as the proper medium of a community which lived together as one family." (Com. Acts of Apos.)

Burkitt says: "Another religious office which they continued constant, was the breaking of bread; that is, receiving the sacrament."

Bengel says: "The Lord's Supper is included in this expression." (Gnomon of New Test.)

Every instance of baptism in the New Testament confirms this view. The first duty after repentance and faith was baptism. As soon as the Samaritans believed the things Philip preached they were baptized both men and women. (Acts 8:12.) The eunuch was baptized at once upon a profession of his faith. (Acts 8:36,37.) As soon as the scales fell from the eyes of Paul he was baptized (Acts 9:18); and the Philipian jailer was baptized the same hour of the night in which he believed. (Acts 16:33.) In none of these cases was there any time to celebrate the Lord's Supper between a profession of faith and baptism.

I read in Acts 20:7: "And upon the first day of the week the disciples came together to break bread, Paul preached unto them, ready to depart on the morrow; and continued his speech until midnight." The Syriac version, and well nigh all commentators agree that this passage refers to the observance of the Lord's Supper. We know that none but disciples were present, for the passage distinctly says this.

Gloag says: "That is to celebrate the Lord's Supper."

Paul in writing to the Corinthian church says: "For first of all when we come together in the church, I hear that there be divisions among you; and I partly believe it. For I have received of the Lord that which also I delivered unto you, That the Lord Jesus the same night in which he

THE BAPTIST POSITION STATED. 33

was betrayed took bread; and when he had given thanks, he brake it, and said, Take, eat; this is my body, which is broken for you: this do in remembrance of me. After the same manner also he took the cup, when he had supped saying, This cup is the new testament in my blood; this do ye, as oft as ye drink it, in remembrance of me. For as often as ye eat this bread, and drink this cup, ye do shew the Lord's death till he come. Wherefore whosoever shall eat this bread, and drink this cup of the Lord, unworthily, shall be guilty of the body and blood of the Lord. But let a man examine himself, and so let him eat of that bread, and drink of that cup."

Paul distinctly says he was addressing the church, verse 18, at Corinth. There is not a word said about outsiders. Indeed the whole of this epistle is in regard to disorderly members in the Corinthian church. This passage proves beyond doubt that the Lord's Supper is a church ordinance.

In chapter 12:12,13 Paul says that baptism precedes the Lord's Supper. Says he: "For as the body is one, and hath many members, and all the members of that one body, being many, are one body; so also is Christ. For by one Spirit are we all baptized into one body, whether we be Jews or Gentiles, whether we be bond or free; and have all been made to drink into one Spirit."

The argument is clear. They have all been

baptized into the one body or church; and they have been made to "drink," or participate of the Lord's Supper, into one Spirit. Bloomfield says of this passage: "This is the interpretation adopted by almost all commentators, ancient and modern, who here suppose an allusion to the two sacraments."

Olshausen says: "The allusion in this passage to x. 1, seq. is unmistakable, so that we may see the *epotistheemen* points to the communion." (Com., vol 4, p. 346.)

Burkitt says: "By baptism we were admitted into his church; and this union of ours, one with another, is testified and declared by our communion at the Lord's table, which is here called a drinking into the Spirit."

Dr. Charles Hodge says: "The allusion is supposed by Luther, Calvin, and Beza to be to the Lord's Supper."

Van Oosterzee, Presbyterian, says: "It is worthy of notice that baptism and the Supper are at least once mentioned by him in one breath, and placed upon a level." (Theol. of New Test., p. 328.)

MacKnight says: "For indeed with the gifts of one Spirit, we all have been baptized into one body, or church, whether Jews or Gentiles, whether slaves or freemen, and all are equally entitled to the privileges of that one body, and derive equal honor from them; and all have been

THE BAPTIST POSITION STATED. 35

made to drink in the Lord's Supper of one Spirit of faith and love, by which the one body is animated."

The priority of baptism to the Lord's Supper is likewise taught in 1 Cor. 10:1-3. The passage reads: "Moreover, brethren, I would not that ye should be ignorant, how that all of our fathers were under the cloud, and all passed through the sea; and were all baptized into Moses in the cloud and in the sea; and did all eat the same spiritual meat; and did all drink the same spiritual drink."

Olshausen says: "Thus in this passage the history of Israel is typically conceived as referring to the sacramental rites of baptism and the Lord's Supper, which contain like holy vessels all the blessings of the gospels; and thus in this very passage lies a powerful argument for these two sacraments." (Com., vol. 4, p. 308.)

Meyer says: "Just as all receive the self same type of baptism (verses 1,2), so too all were partakers of one and the same analogue of the Christian ordinance of the Supper, so that each one therefore stood on the very same level of apparent certainty of not being cast off by God."

Bishop Ellicott says: "The spiritual food referred to was, it hardly need to be said, that which typified one part of the other sacrament."

Godet says: "As the holy Supper serves to maintain in salvation those who have entered into it by the faith professed in baptism, so the Israelites also received, after the initial deliverance, the favors necessary to their preservation. These benefits, corresponding to the bread and wine of the Supper, were the manna daily received, and the water which God caused to issue from a rock in two cases of exceptional distress."

Alford says: "They had what answered to one Christian sacrament, baptism; now the Apostle shows that they were not without a symbolic correspondence to the other, the Lord's Supper."

Dr. Hodge says: "As the miraculous deliverance and miraculous guidance of the Israelites was their baptism, so being miraculously fed was their Lord's Supper."

Stanley says: "This is the natural expression for the voluntary pledge involved in Christian baptism. The food and drink are parallel to the Lord's Supper."

On this point the authorities are conclusive.

From these considerations we think the arguments for baptism as a prerequisite to the Lord's Supper are most conclusive. When once this proposition is admitted our argument is impregnable.

But we can go a step further in this argument. We are not only called upon to obey the ordinances of the Gospel, but we are required to obey them in the divine order. The Scriptures are

THE BAPTIST POSITION STATED. 37

unmistakable on this point. Notice the instructions to the churches.

To the church at Corinth Paul writes: "Wherefore I beseech you be ye followers of me. For this cause have I sent unto you Timotheus, who is my beloved son, and faithful in the Lord, who shall bring you into remembrance of my ways which be in Christ, as I teach everywhere in every church." (1 Cor. 4:16,17.) "Be ye followers of me, even as I am also of Christ. Now I praise you, brethren, that ye remember me in all things, and keep the *ordinances*, as I delivered them to you." (1 Cor. 11:1,2.) "For I have received of the Lord that which I have delivered unto you;" and he immediately gives directions in regard to the Lord's Supper. (1 Cor. 11:23.)

To the church at Philippi: "Brethren, be followers together of me, and mark them which walk so as ye have us for an ensample;" and this exhortation: "Let us walk by the same rule, let us mind the same thing." (Phil. 3:16,17.)

To the church at Colosse: "For though I be absent in the flesh, yet am I with you in the Spirit, judging and beholding your order, and the steadfastness in the faith. Beware lest any man spoil you through philosophy and vain deceit, after the tradition of men, after the rudiments of the world, and not after Christ." (2:5,8.)

To the church at Thessalonica: "Therefore,

brethren, stand fast, and hold the traditions which ye have been taught, whether by word or our epistle." (2 Thes. 2:15.) "And we have confidence in the Lord touching you, that ye both do and will do the things which we command you." (2 Thes. 3:5.)

No comment on these Scriptures is needed. We have no right to vary or change God's commands. He gave us the divine order and we ought to obey him in that order.

CHAPTER III.

THE TESTIMONY OF THE FATHERS.

THE Greek and Latin fathers are quite explicit upon the relative position of baptism and the Lord's Supper. As far as I have observed there is no difference of opinion among them on the subject. I will let them speak for themselves.

Justin Martyr, second century, says: "This food is called among us the eucharist, of which no one is allowed to partake but the man who believes that the things which we teach are true, and who has been washed with the washing that is for the remission of sins, and unto regeneration, and who is so living as Christ has enjoined. For not as common bread and common drink do we receive these." (Apol. 1 c. lxvi. Patrologiæ, Migne, vol. 6, p. 427.)

The second canon of the Council of Antioch, 344, orders that those who came into the church and heard the service, so far as the lections of Scripture, but declined to partake in the prayers of the people or to communicate, should be cast out of the church until they should have professed and repented of their fault." (Canon Apost., c. 9 (10). Hefele's Hist. Councils, vol. 2, p. 67.)

The second Council of Carthage says: "No stranger shall be admitted to receive the communion in another church, without a letter of recommendation from his own bishop." (Hefele's Hist. Coun., vol. 2, p. 187.)

Hippolytus, in the beginning of the third century, in a fragment preserved of his works, makes baptism precede the Lord's Supper. Döllinger also gives this account of a work of Hippolytus: "In a small treatise, in which he castigates and exhorts the Jews, he depicts the marvelous spectacle of Israel pressing, humbled and penitent, to receive baptism, and begging for the food of grace—the Blessed Bread." (Hippolytus and Callistus, p. 319.)

The learned Baron Bunsen, in commenting on Hippolytus and his times, says: "Catechetical instruction, as a general rule, was limited to three years; so that the catechumen, after having completed the first year satisfactorily, might be permitted to hear the Word of God and the sermon; at the conclusion of which, after solemn prayer and the blessing, he was dismissed before the worship of the believers, the service of the general congregation, commenced. Nothing can be more natural; for the celebration of the Lord's Supper was the solemn act of the believers and implied reception into the Christian community, of which it was intended to be the sacred symbol. * * * No one can take part in the solemn ceremony of *a close society*, except one who has been received into it. To have allowed it would have been a contradiction in terms." (Hippolytus and His Age, vol. 2, p. 108.)

Cyril of Jerusalem, 347, says: "After the baptism followed the holy communion, of which all the newly baptized were partakers, therein becoming 'of one body and of one blood' and there partaking of a heavenly bread, and of a cup of salvation, that sanctify both soul and body." (Myst. Catch. iv. Patrologiæ, vol. 33, p. 1102.)

Origin says: "It doth not belong to every one to eat of this bread, and to drink of this cup." (Com. in Joan., vol. 2, p. 345.)

Jerome, the most learned of the fathers, 400, says: "Catechumens cannot communicate at the Lord's table, being unbaptized." (Patrologiæ, vol. 22, p. 658.)

Augustine, 400, speaking of administering baptism to infants, says: "Of which certainly they cannot partake unless they are baptized." (Animadversiones t. ii. Also De Pecat. Remiss. lib. i.)

The Didache says: "But let no one eat or drink of your eucharist, except those baptized into the name of the Lord; for as regards this also the Lord has said: Give not that which is holy to the dogs." (Didache, C. ix, sec. 5.)

In the Recognitions of Clement I read: "For he who wished soon to be baptized is separated but a little time, but he for a longer who wishes to be baptized later. Every one therefore has it in his own power to demand a shorter or longer time for his repentance; and therefore it lies with you, when you wish it, to come to our table; and not with us, who are not permitted to take food with any one who has not been baptized." (Recog., B. ii, C. lxxii. Patrologiæ, vol. 1, p. 1282.)

The Apostolic Constitutions say: "But if he afterwards repents, and turns from his error, then, as we receive the heathen, when they wish to repent, into the church indeed to hear the word, but do not receive them to communion until they have received the seal of baptism, and are made complete Christians; so we do not permit such as these to enter only to hear, until they show the fruit of repentance, that by hearing the word they may not utterly and irrevocably be lost." (Apos. Con., B. 2, sec. 5, c. xxxix. Patrologiæ, vol. 1, p. 694.)

Dr. Philip Schaff commenting on this says that the Apostolic Constitutions "lay great stress on the exclusion of unbelievers from the eucharist." (Teaching, p. 193.)

Jobius says: "We are baptized, annointed, and then thought worthy of the precious blood." (Döllinger's Hist. Christ. Ch., vol. 2, p. 324.)

In the life of Basil it is recorded that: "Maximus, the bishop, baptized him an Eubulus, and clothed them with white garments, and, annointing them with the holy chrism, gave them the communion." (Amphiloch., vit. Basil, cap. v.)

Tertullian, the first of the Latin fathers, says: "To deal with this matter briefly, I shall begin with baptism. When we are going to enter the water, but a little before, in the presence of the congregation, and under the hand of the president, we solemnly profess that we disown the devil, and his pomp, and his angels. Hereupon we are thrice immersed, making a somewhat ampler pledge than the Lord has appointed in the gospel. * * * Then we also, in congregations before daybreak, and from the hand of none but the president, receive the sacrament of the eucharist, which the Lord both commanded to be eaten at meal times, and enjoined to be taken by all alike." (De Corona, c. 3. Patrologiæ, vol. 1, p. 98.)

Bede, A. D. 613, says: "If you will be baptized into the salutary fountain as your father was, you may also partake of the Lord's Supper as he did; but if you despise the former, ye cannot in any wise receive the latter." (Eccl. Hist., lib. ii, cap. v. Patrologiæ, vol. 95.)

Theophylact, A. D. 1100, says: "No unbaptized person partakes of the Lord's Supper." (On Math. 14.)

Bonaventura, 1200, says: "Faith, indeed, is necessary to all of the sacraments, but especially to the reception of baptism, because baptism is the first among the sacraments." (Apud Forbesium, Instruct. Historic. Theolog., lib x, cap. iv. 9.)

We can reach the same conclusion that baptism precedes communion from another standpoint. The word mass, which is now used to designate the communion in the Catholic church, originated in the ancient church, in the dismissal of the unbaptized from the congregation before the observance of the Lord's Supper. Dr. Schaff says of this word: "The name *missa* (from which our mass is derived) occurs first in Augustine and in the acts of the council of Carthage, A. D. 398. It arose from the formula of dismission at the close of each part of the service, and is equivalent to *missio, dismissio*. Augustine (Serm. 49, c. 8): 'Take notice, after the sermon, the dismissal (*missa*) of the catechumens takes place; the faithful will remain.' Afterwards *missa* came to designate exclusively the communion service. In the Greek church *leitourgia* or *litourgia*, service, is the precise equivalent of *missa*." (Hist. Christ. Ch., vol. 2, p. 232, note.)

But we need not appeal to Dr. Schaff, as we have the original authorities before us. Thus, by the Council of Carthage, 398: "That the bishop forbid no one to enter the church and hear the Word of God, be he Gentile, or heretic, or Jew, until the dismissal (*missam*) of the catechumens." (Can. 84.) Augustine about the same time makes a similar statement as I have quoted from Dr. Schaff. Cassia, A. D. 424, speaks of one who was overheard while alone to preach a sermon, and then to "give out the dismissal of the catechumens as the deacon does." (Coenob. Instit., xi. 15.) The Council of Valentia, 524: "That the gospel be read before the mass of the catechumens." (Can. 1.) The Council of Lerida in the same year decreed that persons living in incest should be allowed to remain in the church only to the mass of the catechumens." (Can. 4.) The formula of dismission in the Latin church was: "If there be any catechumens here let them go out." (Scudmore's Notitia Eucharista, p. 336, ed. 2.)

The Apostolic Constitutions read: "But let them not be admitted to communion in prayer; and let them depart after the reading of the law, and the prophets, and the Gospel, that by such departure they may be made better in their course of life, by endeavoring to meet every day about the public assemblies, and to be frequent in prayer, that they may at length be admitted, and that those who behold them may be affected, and be more secured by fearing to fall into the same condition." (B. ii, c. xl.)

Lyman Coleman, a noted Presbyterian Archæologist, says upon this passage: "It appears from the Apostolic Constitutions, that after the doors had been carefully closed and a guard set, the deacon made a public proclamation of the different classes of persons who were not permitted to be present on the occasion. These were the first and second classes of catechumens, the unbelievers, Jews and pagans, and reputed heretics and separatists of every description. The penitents and inergumens are not here mentioned, but it appears from other sources that they were not permitted to be present at the Lord's table. None indeed but believers in full communion with the church were permitted to be present. All such, originally, partook of the sacrament." (Antiq. Christ. Ch., pp. 308, 309.)

The above extracts prove conclusively that the unbaptized were not permitted at the Lord's Supper. The most scholarly writers admit that this was the practice of the primitive church.

Prof. Samuel Cheetham, Episcopalian, says: "Conditions of admission to holy communion. Communicants must be baptized persons, not under censure. None could be admitted to holy communion but baptized persons lying under no censure. The competency of ordinary members of the church would be known as a matter of course to the clergy administering the sacrament. Persons from a distance were required to produce certificates from their own bishops that they were in the peace of the church, before they could be admitted to holy communion. Some have thought that the expression *communio peregrina* designates the state of those strangers who, being unprovided with such letters, were admitted to be present at divine service, but not to communicate." (Dict. Christ. Antiq., vol. 1, p. 417.)

Bishop Stillingfleet, Episcopalian, says: *Missa* "was then only taken for the public service of the church, so called from the dismission of the people after it, with an *Ite, missa est;* and from the different forms of Christians, they had two several services, the one called *missa catechumenorum*, because at the end of that the catechumens were dismissed from the assembly; the other *missa fidelium*, at which they received the Lord's Supper; which afterwards, (the former discipline of the church decaying), engrossed the name *missa* to itself." (Irenecum, p. 263.)

Lord Chancellor King, Episcopalian, says: "Hence when other parts of divine worship were ended, and the celebration of the eucharist was to begin, the catechumens, penitents, and all, except the communicants, were to depart, as Tertullian says thereof: 'Pious initiations drive away the profane.' These being mysteries which were to be kept secret and concealed from all, except the faithful." (Prim. Ch., p. 243.)

Döllinger, Catholic, says: "The doors of the church were now closed, and the mass of the faithful, who alone remained within, commenced: it consisted of three parts, the offertory, the consecration, and the communion." (Hist. Christ. Ch., vol. 2, p. 310.)

Kurtz, Lutheran, says: "In connection with the arrangements about the catechumens, public worship was divided into *missa catechumenorum* and a *missa fidelium*. From the latter, all who had not been baptized, who were under discipline, or were possessed by an unclean spirit, were excluded." (Church Hist., vol. 1, p. 121.)

Neander, Lutheran, says: "With reference to these two constituent portions of the church assemblies, the catechumens and baptized believers, the whole service was divided into two portions: one in which the catechumens were allowed to join, embracing the reading of the Scriptures and the sermon, the prevailing didactic portion; and the other, in which the baptized alone could take part, embracing whatever was designated to represent the fellowship of believers—communion, and all the prayers of the church which preceded it." (Hist. Christ. Ch., vol. 2, pp. 324, 325.)

Guericke, Lutheran, says: "The service was preceded by the call of the deacon, excluding catechumens, and all unbelievers, heretics, hypocrites, unreconciled persons, etc., from participating in it." (Manual of Ch. Hist., p. 302.)

Dr. Schaff, Presbyterian, says: "The public service was divided from the middle of the second century down to the close of the fifth, into the worship of the catechumens, and the worship of the faithful. The former consisted of Scripture reading, preaching, prayer and song and was open to the unbaptized and persons under penance. The latter consisted of the holy communion, with its liturgical appendages; none but the proper members of the church could attend it; and before it began, all catechumens and unbelievers left the assembly at the order of the deacon, and the doors were closed and guarded." (Hist. Christ. Ch., vol. 2, p. 232.)

Here we have the unanimous authority of the Fathers that no one was permitted to participate in the Lord's Supper who had not been baptized and was a member of the church in good standing. The celebrated rule of Augustine is in point. He says: "What the whole church, through all the world does practice, and yet has not been instituted in councils, but has been always in use, is with very good reason supposed to have been settled by the authority of the apostles." (Wall's Hist. Infant Bapt., vol. 1, p. 85.) The conclusions from this rule are perfect. No one in all antiquity denies that baptism and church membership preceded the Lord's Supper.

CHAPTER IV.

THE TESTIMONY OF SCHOLARS.

SCHOLARS of every denomination testify to our position that baptism precedes the Lord's Supper. There is so much material at hand, and so many eminent men to select from, that I am embarrassed in having to choose a few witnesses. These men represent the scholarship of the world, and are worthy of a hearing. I present,

1. Writers upon history. There is not a standard historian, who speaks upon the subject, that does not testify that baptism precedes the Lord's Supper. Moreover *there is not a standard historian who gives any account of open communion for the first sixteen hundred years after Christ.* But I shall let the historians speak.

The German writers will lead.

Mosheim says: "Neither those doing penance, nor those not yet baptized, were allowed to be present at the celebration of this ordinance." (Eccl. Hist., vol. 1, p. 189.)

Neander says: "At this celebration, as may be easily concluded, no one could be present who was not a member of the Christian church, and incorporated into it by the rite of baptism." (Church Hist., vol. 1, p. 271.)

THE TESTIMONY OF SCHOLARS. 51

Gieseler says: "The eucharist was considered the symbol of the intimate communion of the church with Christ and one another." (Ch. Hist., vol. 1, p. 104.)

Kurtz says: "All unbaptized persons were excluded." (Church Hist., vol. 1, p. 123.)

A brilliant Frenchman testifies.

Pressensè says: "While the Lord's Supper was thus celebrated with all simplicity and liberty, it was, nevertheless, with much solemnity in the eyes of the church. It summed up in one symbol, chosen by the Lord himself, the whole Christian religion. To partake of it was to make the most solemn profession of faith in Christ. To receive it unworthily was not only to despise the Lord's body in the symbol which spiritually set it forth, but also to make the church partaker in the sin. Thus serious and severe discipline was appointed not merely to prevent the profanation of the Lord's Supper, but also to repress all kinds of irregularities." (Early Years of Christianity, p. 379.)

Here is a voice from Switzerland.

Frederick Spanheim says: "The oblation of the eucharistical bread and wine by the people followed; the consecration of it by prayer, and the distribution to the faithful and baptized in remembrance of the death of Christ." (Eccl. Annals, p. 177.)

I put an infidel on the stand.

Gibbon says: "One circumstance may be observed, in which the modern churches have materially departed from the ancient custom. The sacrament of baptism (even when it is administered to infants) was immediately followed by confirmation and the holy communion." (Decline and Fall of the Roman Empire, vol. 2, p. 271.)

Old England testifies.

Milman says: "Baptism, or the initiation into the Christian community, was a solemn ceremonial, requiring previous examination and probation. The governing power would possess and exercise the authority to admit into the community. They would perform, or, at all events, superintend the initiatory rite of baptism. The other distinctive rite of Christianity, the celebration of the Lord's Supper, would require a more active interference and co-operation on the part of those who presided over the community." (History Christ., p. 198.)

J. G. Robertson says: "None were admitted but such as were baptized and in full communion with the church." (Hist. Christ. Ch., vol. 1, p. 168.)

Waddington says: "The sacraments of the primitive church were two—baptism and the Lord's Supper." (Hist. Ch., p. 46.)

Homersham Cox says: "From a subsequent passage it appears that immediately after baptism, the convert was brought into the congregation, and partook of the eucharist." (First Cent Christ., p. 278.)

The scholarship of America joins all the rest.

Professor Fisher, Congregationalist, says: "Toward the close of the second century we find it to be the custom to exclude non-communicants from being present at the Lord's Supper. After the preliminary services, at the close of the addresses of the bishop and presbyters, the unbaptized were dismissed. From the Latin word signifying dismissal (*missa*) the word mass is derived." (Hist. Christ. Ch., p. 66.)

Gregory and Ruter, Methodists, say: "With respect to the few and simple rites instituted by Christ, it appears, that the sacrament of the Lord's Supper was administered, by the first Christians, whenever they assembled for the purposes of social worship; and so far from being confined to those who had made the greatest progress in religious attainments, it was equally participated in by the apostle of Christ and the meanest member of the church. The initiatory rite of baptism was usually performed, by immersing the whole body in the baptismal font, and in the earlier periods of Christianity was permitted to all who acknowledged the truths of the Gospel, and promised conformity to its laws. The introduction of unworthy and disorderly persons into the church, from easiness of admission, naturally narrowed the terms of communion, and baptism was afterwards confined to those who had been previously instructed in religious knowledge, and proved the sincerity of their professions by the regularity of their lives. The probationers for admission into the society of Christians took the humble name of Catechumens, while those who were already consecrated by baptism were distinguished by the superior title of Believers." (Church Hist., pp. 33, 34.)

Dr. Schaff, Presbyterian, says: "The two sacraments of baptism and the Lord's Supper, the antetypes of circumcision and the passover under the Old Testament, were instituted by Christ as efficatious signs, pledges, and means of the grace of the new covenant. They are related to each other as regeneration and sanctification, or as the beginning and growth of the Christian life." (Hist. Christ. Ch., vol. 1, p. 465.)

Surely the Baptists must be right when all history gives such a willing voice to their position.

2. Writers upon the church. These writers have studied the church and her ordinances from every conceivable standpoint, and yet, wonderful to say, on this point they are unanimous.

Litton, Episcopalian, says: "To his church, represented in the apostles, he delivered the sacraments. Believers are to be baptized in the name of the Father, Son, and Holy Ghost; baptized Christians are to eat the bread and drink the cup, and thus to feed spiritually upon his body and blood. These simple directions comprise all of the particulars of the original institution." (The Church of Christ, p. 156.)

Jacob, Episcopalian, says: The baptized person "was at once admitted to the Lord's Supper, which was commonly administered to newly baptized infants, as well as to those of riper years." (Eccl. Pol. of New Test., p. 279.)

Bishop Kaye, Episcopalian, says: "Christ himself instituted two rites—the one to be the outward mode of initiation—the other the outward mark of communion with it." (Exter. Govern. and Discipline of the Church, p. 30.)

Dr. Killen, Presbyterian, says: "As baptism was designed to supercede the Jewish circumcision, the Lord's Supper was intended to occupy the place of the Jewish Passover. The Paschal lamb could be sacrificed nowhere except in the Temple of Jerusalem, and the passover was kept only once a year; but the eucharist could be dispensed wherever a Christian congregation was collected." (The Ancient Ch., p. 218.)

Bannerman, Presbyterian, says: "Baptism, as commonly administered, to entrants into the church, takes infeftment, so to speak, of our flesh when we enter into covenant with Christ, that not even the lower part of our being may be left without the attestation that he has redeemed it. The Lord's Supper, as administered from time to time to those who have been admitted into the church before, renews this infeftment at intervals, and attests that the covenant by which we are Christ's still holds good both for the body and the spirit which He has ransomed in Himself." (The Church of Christ, vol. 2, p. 129.)

3. Writers on Systematic Theology and Dogmatics. These men have given their lives to the direct study of the Scriptures, and their testimony is important.

Turretin, Presbyterian, says: "It is one thing to have a right to these external ordinances of the church, which belong to a profession; it is another thing to be interested in the internal blessings of faith. Unbaptized believers have actually a right to these, because they are already partakers of Christ and his benefits; though they have not yet a right to those, except in observing the appointed order of baptism." (Institut. Theol., Tom iii, Loc. xviii, Quaes. iv, § 10, p. 22.)

Mastricht says: "As no uncircumcised male was admitted to the typical supper, that is the passover; so, under the New Testament, no unbaptized person is admitted to the Lord's table." (Theol., lib. vii, cap. v, § 29.)

Pictetus, Presbyterian, says: "The Supper of our Lord ought not to be administered to persons that are unbaptized: for before baptism, men are not considered as members of the visible church." (Theolog. Christiana, pp. 959, 960.)

THE TESTIMONY OF SCHOLARS. 57

Marckius says: "The dying and the unbaptized, are not to be admitted to communion." (Compend. Theolog. Christ., p. 604.)

Witsius says: "For as two things are required to complete our happiness: first, our being absolved from our sins, and washed from our pollution; that we may be regenerated by the communication of the Spirit of Christ to a new life of grace, that is sustained, strengthened and increased therein, until we be promoted to the life of glory both these are sufficiently confirmed to us by these two sacraments. Our first engrafting into Christ, and our regeneration by the Spirit, are set forth by baptism; and the nourishment of our spiritual life by the holy supper." (Econ. Cov., vol. 2, p. 421.)

Dr. Dabney, Southern Presbyterian, says: "That the sacrament is to be given only to credible professors, does not indeed follow necessarily from the fact that it symbolizes saving grace; for baptism does this; but from the express limitation of Paul, and from the different graces symbolized. Baptism symbolizes those graces which initiate the Christian life: the Supper, those also which continue it." (Sys. Polem. Theol., pp. 803, 804.)

Dr. McDowell, Presbyterian, says: "The qualifications to come to the Lord's Supper, in sight of the church ought to be visible piety. For the officers in the church, cannot search the heart;

but they ought to look for evidence of that which God requires, which has been shown to be real piety. And since they have had committed to them by Christ, the keys of the visible kingdom, with power to open and shut it, it becomes them to examine persons applying to be received to the Lord's Supper, to enable them to form a judgment whether they possess or not the requisite qualifications." (Theol., vol. 2, pp. 511, 512.)

Dr. Martensen, bishop in Denmark, says: "Baptism is the setting up of the new covenant; the Lord's Supper is its renewal. By baptism a man is incorporated into the new kingdom, and the possibility of, the necessary requirements for, the new personality are given therein; by means of the Lord's Supper this new personality is brought to perfection. * * * The Lord's Supper as a church ordinance, must be looked upon as an act of confession, appointed by the Lord to refresh our remembrance of him." (Christ. Dogmat., p. 432.)

4. Writers on Christian Antiquities. Writers on this subject are supposed to weigh all kinds of testimony, and had there been any deviation on this subject they would undoubtedly have mentioned it.

Riddle, Episcopalian, says: "In the primitive church, the eucharist was administered immediately after baptism to persons newly admitted into the church by that rite; who, it is to be remembered, were adults, and had gone through a preparatory course of instruction." "According to the original laws and customs of the church, the communicants consisted of all persons who had been admitted as members of the church by baptism." (Christ. Antiq., p. 572.)

Coleman, Presbyterian, says: "Agreeably to all the laws and customs of the church, baptism constituted membership with the church. All baptized persons were legitimately numbered among the communicants, as members of the church. Accordingly the sacrament immediately followed the ordinance of baptism, that the members thus received might come at once into the enjoyment of all the rights and privileges of Christian fellowship." (Antiq. Christ. Ch., pp. 309, 310.)

Guericke says: "At a very early date it was the custom, immediately after the act of baptism," to admit the candidate "with the rest of the church to the Holy Communion." (Manual Antiq. Ch., pp. 233, 236.)

5. Miscellaneous writers.

Ravenellius says: "Baptism ought to precede; nor is the holy Supper to be administered to any, except they be baptized." (Bibliotheca Sacra, tom. i, p. 301.)

Zanchius says: "We believe that baptism, as a sacrament appointed by Christ, is absolutely necessary to the church." (Opera, tom. viii, p. 416.)

Hornbekius says: "No one is admitted to the sacred supper unless he is baptized." (Socin. Confut., tom. ii, p. 416.)

Dr. Manton says: "Before the church, none but baptized persons have a right to the Lord's table." (Supplem. Morn. Exercis., p. 199.)

Dr. Green, Presbyterian, says: "It appears from several passages of the New Testament, that baptism and the Lord's Supper in the Christian church, have succeeded to circumcision and the passover in the Jewish." (Lect. Shorter Cat., vol. 2, p. 358.)

Dr. Stier says: "Yet it must be maintained, with Luther, that the forgiveness of sins is also imparted in the Gospel, as here, through the word; we may say, further, that the first sacrament, baptism, had already communicated forgiveness to the participants of the Supper." (Words of Lord Jesus, vol. 7, p. 135.)

Surely the Baptists must be right on the Lord's Supper when their position is thus heartily endorsed by the scholarship of the world. From whatever standpoint we view the subject the conclusion is the same. All scholars concede that baptism must precede the Lord's Supper. The man, therefore, who rants about Baptist "close communion" must be ignorant of the scholarship of the world, or hopelessly blinded by prejudice.

CHAPTER V.

THE TESTIMONY OF CREEDS, CONFESSIONS, ETC.

I HAVE put myself to much trouble to look through the creeds of various sects, Roman Catholic and Protestant, and they all lay down the order claimed by the Baptists. This is important testimony. It shows that the whole Christian world is a unit on this important point. The order we claim, and the creeds admit, is that baptism precedes the Lord's Supper.

The Roman Catholics are very clear on this point. The Council of Trent, 1547, has: "Baptism, Confirmation, the Eucharist." (De Sacramentis in Genere., can. 1.) The Profession of the Tridentine Faith, 1564, has the same. (See Bulls of Pope Pius IV., Injunctum Nobis, November 13th, 1564.)

The Orthodox Eastern, or Greek Church, has: "Baptism, Unction with Chrism, Communion." (Queas. xcviii, Longer Cat. Eastern Church.)

The Old Catholic Church has: "Baptism and the eucharist." (Fourteen Theses Old Catholic Union, Bonn, Art. IX.)

The First Helvetic Confession, A. D. 1536, Swiss Divines, Bullinger and others, Art. XXI: "Baptism and the eucharist."

The Second Helvetic Confession, 1566: "Baptism and the Supper of the Lord." (Art. XIX.)

The Heidelberg Catechism, 1563, question 68: "How many sacraments has Christ appointed in the New Testament? Answer. Two: holy baptism and the holy supper."

The Belgic Confession, 1561: "Moreover, we are satisfied with the number of sacraments which Christ our Lord hath instituted, which are two only, namely, the Sacrament of Baptism, and the Holy Supper of our Lord Jesus Christ." (Art. XXIII.)

The Scotch Confession of Faith, 1560: "As the Father is under the law, besides the veritie of the Sacrifices, had twa chiefe Sacraments, to wit, Circumcision and the Passover, the despisers and contemners whereof were not reputed for God's people: sa do we acknowledge and confesse that we now in the time of the Evangell have twa chiefe Sacraments, onelie instituted be the Lord Jesus, and commanded to be used of all they that will be reputed members of this body, to wit, Baptisme and the Supper or Table of the Lord Jesus, called the Communion of his body and his blude." (Art. XXI.)

The Thirty-nine Articles of the Church of England, 1563, 1571, 1801: "There are two sacraments ordained of Christ our Lord in the Gospel, that is to say, Baptism and the Supper of the Lord. (Art. XXV.)

The Irish articles of religion, 1615: "There be two sacraments ordained of Christ our Lord in the Gospel; that is to say: Baptism and the Lord's Supper." (Sect. 85.)

The Westminster Confession, 1647: "There be only two sacraments ordained by Christ our Lord in the Gospel, that is to say, Baptism and the Supper of the Lord: neither of which may be dispensed by any but by a minister of the Word lawfully ordained." (Art. XXVII.)

The Methodist, 1784: "There are two sacraments ordained of Christ our Lord in the Gospel; that is to say, Baptism and the Supper of the Lord." (Art. XVI.)

Our position must be a very strong one when all of the Creeds of Christendom endorse it. We hold in common with all others that baptism precedes the Lord's Supper.

CHAPTER VI.

THE TERMS OF COMMUNION IN THE EPISCOPAL CHURCH. ARE THE EPISCOPALIANS CLOSE COMMUNIONISTS?

WE can undoubtedly answer this question in the affirmative. The Episcopalians are quite strict in their requirements. We notice:

1. The Episcopalians declare that baptism and church membership precede communion.

Prof. Cheetham, Professor of Pastoral Theology in King's College, London, says: "None could be admitted to holy communion but baptized persons lying under no censure." (Dict. Antiq., vol. 1, p. 417.)

The Episcopal *Recorder* says: "The close communion of the Baptist churches is but the necessary sequence of the fundamental idea out of which their existence has grown. No Christian church would willingly receive to its communion even the humblest and truest believer in Christ who had not been baptized. With Baptists, immersion only is baptism, and they therefore of necessity exclude from the Lord's table all who have not been immersed. It is an essential part of the system—the legitimate carrying out of the creed."

THE EPISCOPALIANS. 65

Dr. Wall says: "For no church ever gave the communion to any persons before they were baptized. * * * Since among all of the absurdities that ever were held, none ever maintained that, any person should partake of the communion before he was baptized." (Wall's Hist. Infant Bapt., vol. 1, pp. 632, 638.)

Lord Chancellor King says: "As for the persons communicating, they were not indifferently all that professed the Christian faith, as Origin writes: 'It doth not belong to every one to eat of the bread, and to drink of this cup.' But they were only such as were in the number of the faithful, 'such as were baptized, and received both the credentials and practices of Christianity.' That is, who believe the articles of the Christian faith, and led a holy and pious life. Such as these, and none else, were permitted to communicate. Now since none but the faithful were admitted, it follows that the catechumens and the penitents were excluded; the catechumens, because they were not yet baptized, for baptism always preceded the Lord's Supper." (Prim. Ch., pp. 242, 243.)

Bingham says: "Now the obligation which every man laid upon himself in baptism, as we have shown in a former book, was the profession and actual performance of three things: 1. Repentance, or a renunciation of all former sin, together with the author of it, the devil. 2. Faith, or belief of the several articles of the Christian institution or mystery of godliness. 3. A holy and constant obedience paid to the laws of this holy religion. In the performance of which sincerely and without dissimulation, every man was supposed to be truly qualified for baptism; and what qualified him for baptism, also qualified him for the communion; of which there is this certain evidence, that as soon as any man was baptized, he was immediately communicated; which could not regularly have been done, but upon presumption, that he that was duly qualified for baptism was qualified for communion." (Origines Eccl., vol. 2, p. 835.)

Dr. Cave says: "The communicants in the primitive church were those that embraced the doctrine of the gospel, and had been baptized into the faith of Christ. For looking upon the Lord's Supper as the highest and most solemn act of religion, they thought they could never take care enough in the dispensing of it." (Prim. Christ., P. 1, c. xi, p. 333.)

That the Baptists are consistent in their terms of communion these authors frankly admit.

2. The Episcopalians have put around the Lord's Table the most stringent rules.

(1). It is required by Episcopalians that the minister who administers the communion must be Episcopally ordained. The XXXIII Article reads: "It is not lawful for any man to take upon him the office of public preaching, or ministering the sacraments in the congregation, before he be lawfully called and sent to execute the same: and these we ought to judge lawfully called and sent, which be chosen and called to this work by men who have public authority given unto them in the congregation to call and send ministers into the Lord's vineyard."

What is meant by "lawful authority"? Rev. Henry Cary says: "The Church of England ever upheld the necessity of an Apostolic succession, and Episcopal ordination. For, to use the expressions introductory to ordination service, 'it is evident unto all men diligently reading the Holy Scripture and ancient authors, that from the Apostles' time there have been these orders of ministers in Christ's Church, Bishops, Priests, and Deacons, which officers were evermore had in such reverend estimation, that no man might presume to execute any of them, except he were first called, tried, examined, and known to have such qualities as are requisite for the same; and also by public prayer with imposition of hands by lawful authority. And therefore, to the intent that these orders may be continued, and reverently used and esteemed, in the United Church of England and Ireland, and no man shall be accounted or taken to be a lawful Bishop, Priest or Deacon, in the United Church of England and Ireland, or suffered to execute any of the said functions, except he be called, tried, examined, and admitted thereunto, according to the form hereafter following, or hath had formal Episcopal consecration or ordination." (Test. Fathers, pp. 275, 276.)

That is plain enough. According to the Thirty-nine Articles no Baptist, Methodist, Presbyterian, or other schismatic has a right to administer the Lord's Supper. The Episcopalian clergyman who would participate in an open communion ceremony with a Methodist or Presbyterian congregation would violate the fundamental law of the Episcopal church.

(2.) Schismatics, that is to say Baptists, Methodists or Presbyterians, are to be excluded from the Episcopal table. Charles Wheatly, and there is no higher authority on the Prayer Book, says: "But besides persons excommunicated, and those above mentioned (disorderly and unbaptized), there are other persons, by the laws of our church, disabled from communicating: such are of course, all schismatics, to whom no minister, when he celebrates the communion, is wittingly to administer the same, under pain of suspension." (Wheatly on Book of Common Prayer, p. 261.)

There is no doubt about that being close communion.

(3.) The Episcopalians demand that a man shall be confirmed, or desirous of being confirmed, before he can sit down to their communion. At the close of the rubric on Confirmation the Prayer Book says: "And there shall none be admitted to the Holy Communion, until such a time as he be confirmed, or be ready and desirous to be confirmed."

Wake, Dean of Canterbury, says: "Is there anything further required of those who come to the Lord's Supper? A. Yes, there is; that they may first be confirmed by the bishop." (The Princ. Christ. Relig. Explained, p. 374.)

Bishop Williams, Connecticut, says: "No member of any religious society, outside of the church, can receive her holy communion without a violation of a fundamental law of the liturgy; and no clergyman can administer it to such a person without a violation of his ordination vows. The rubric commands that no person shall be admitted to the holy communion until they have been, or are ready to be confirmed."

Dr. W. A. Snively says: Confirmation "has constant reference to the baptismal vow, to the promises then made, and the system of instruction then prescribed; and it looks forward to the admission of the candidate to his full privilege, as a member of Christ, in the Holy Communion." (Parish Lect. on Book of Prayer, p. 214.)

Charles Wheatly says: "By a rubric at the end of the order of Confirmation, none are to be admitted to the Holy Communion, until such a time as he be confirmed, or be ready and desirous to be confirmed. The like provision is made by our provincial Constitutions, which allow none to communicate (unless at the point of death), but such as are confirmed, or at least have a reasonable impediment for not being confirmed; and the Glossary allows no impediment to be reasonable, but the want of a bishop near the place." (Book Com. Prayer, p. 262.)

These rules are such that no Baptist, Methodist, Presbyterian, could sit down at the Episcopal table, as they are not ready nor desirous of being confirmed.

(4.) Episcopalians will not even commune with transient Episcopalians. Wheatley says: "All strangers from other parishes; the minister is by the canons required to forbid and to remit such home to their own parish churches and ministers, there to receive the Communion with the rest of their neighbors." (Book Com. Prayer, p. 262.)

(5.) The Episcopal rules require that no evil liver shall be permitted to commune at the Lord's table. The English Prayer Book reads: "If among those who come to be partakers of the Holy Communion, the minister shall know any to be open and notorious evil livers, or to have done any wrong to his neighbors by word or deed, so that the Congregation be thereby offended; he shall advertize him, that he presume not to come to the Lord's table, until he have openly declared himself to have truly repented and amended his former evil life, that the Congregation may thereby be satisfied; and that he hath recompensed the parties to whom he hath done wrong; or at least declared himself to be in full purpose to do so, as soon as he conveniently may."

This rubric has been omitted from the liturgy of the American church, but is regarded as binding; in some of the States a canon to this effect is enacted and in full force. T. C. Brownwell, D.D., LL.D., Bishop of Connecticut, says: "This Rubric has been omitted by our American Revisers of the Liturgy; probably from the inconvenience of conveying the notice in our scattered Congregations. But it is desirable that there should be a general direction, requiring all persons to advertize the minister of their wishes, before presenting themselves to the Holy Table for the first time. This is probably now the general usage of the Church. There is also a canon to this effect in the Diocese of Connecticut, and there may perhaps be similar Canons in some of the other Dioceses. But the general regulations of the Church are paramount to any local injunctions." (Book of Com. Prayer, p. 360.)

(6.) Episcopalians permit no person who holds malice to come to their table. In the Administration of the Lord's Supper, the Prayer Book says: "The same order shall the minister use with those, betwixt whom he perceiveth malice and hatred to reign; not suffering them to be partakers of the Lord's Supper, until he know them to be reconciled."

(7.) Episcopalians practice close communion in the burial of the dead. Under that head the Prayer Book says: "Here it is to be noted, that the office ensuing is not to be used for any unbaptized adults, any who die excommunicated, or who have laid violent hands upon themselves."

(8.) In order to commune with the Episcopalians you must endorse the whole book of Common Prayer. The Constitutions and Canons, No. 4, say: "Whosoever shall hereafter affirm, that the form of God's Worship contained in the Book of Common Prayer and administration of the Sacraments, containeth anything in it that is repugnant to the Scriptures, let him be excommunicated *ipso facto*, and not restored but by the bishop of the place, or archbishop, after his repentance and public revocation of such wicked errors."

In corroboration of all that I have said, I give the testimony of two leading bishops of the Episcopal Church. I asked the following questions: "Does the Episcopal Church require a godly life as a prerequisite to the Lord's Supper? Does it require Baptism? Does it require Confirmation? Does it require Church membership? Any other prerequisites?" The answer was plain and clear.

Bishop Hugh Miller Thompson, LL.D., of Mississippi, says:

BATTLE HILL, JACKSON, MISS., May 7, 1892.
MR. J. T. CHRISTIAN:

Dear Sir: In reply to your enquiries of May 4th, just come to my hands, I beg to say: To Question 1st: Decidedly yes—"a sober, righteous, and godly life." To Question 2nd: Yes, invariably. To Question 3rd: Not always. Reasons and explanations in the Confirmation ritual. To Question 4th: Yes. Baptism makes one a member of the Church. A man communicates because he is a member of the Household. It is a Family Table.

No other requirements save, Faith and Repentance and Prayerful resolutions to live a sober, righteous and godly life. I answer your questions in order, supposing you have retained a copy.

The Prayer Book is our best explanation, however. Very truly yours,
HUGH MILLER THOMPSON.

The Rt. Rev. T. U. Dudley, S. T. D., Bishop of Kentucky, says:

LOUISVILLE, KY., 716 Third St., May 16, 1892.
MR. J. T. CHRISTIAN, Jackson, Miss.

My Dear Sir: I write hurriedly as I am obliged to do in reply to your letter of the 13th.

1. The Rubric in the Communion office of the

Prayer Book says: "If among those who come to be partakers of the communion the minister shall know any to be open and notorious evil livers, or to have done any wrong to his neighbors by word or deed, so that the congregation be thereby offended: he shall advertize him, that he presume not to come to the Lord's table, until he have openly declared himself to have truly repented and amended his former evil life, that the congregation may thereby be satisfied; and that he hath recompensed the parties to whom he hath done wrong: or at least declare himself to be in full purpose so to do as soon as he conveniently may."

2. We do require baptism.

3. That a person may become a regular communicant of the church confirmation is required.

4. All baptized persons are members of the church, and so of course as no unbaptized person may receive the Holy Communion, only church members may do so.

I am truly yours,
T. U. DUDLEY, Bishop of Kentucky.

Instead of being one of open communion, the history of the Episcopal Church is one of bloodshed and persecution. Henry VIII. was scarcely established as head of the Episcopal Church till he began to persecute the Baptists. In 1535, according to the old Chronicler Stow: "On the

THE EPISCOPALIANS. 75

25th day of May, in St. Paul's Church, London, nineteen men and six women, born in Holland, who held that the children of infidel parents might be saved; that the baptism of infants is of none effect; that the elements, the bread and the wine, in the Lord's Supper, remain unchanged, and are bread and wine still, were ordered to be examined and their views condemned. Fourteen of the twenty-five were condemned to suffer death, one man and one woman were condemned to be burned in Smithfield, and the others were sent to other towns to be burnt." (Stow's Chronicle, p. 576.)

Froude, the historian, says of these people: "The details are gone—their names are gone. Poor Hollanders they were, and that is all. Scarcely the fact seemed worthy of the mention, so shortly is it told in a passing paragraph. For them no Europe was agitated, no courts were ordered into mourning, no papal hearts trembled with indignation. At their death the world looked on complacent, indifferent or exulting. Yet here, too, out of twenty-five poor men and women were found fourteen who, by no terror of stake or torture, could be tempted to say they believed what they did not believe. History for them has no word of praise; yet they, too, were not giving their blood in vain. Their lives might have been as useless as the lives of the most of us. In their death they assisted to pay the purchase-money for England's freedom."

In 1536, the King and Convocation set forth articles against the Baptists, of which I present the following:

"1. Infants must needs be christened, because they be born in original sin; which sin must needs be remitted: which cannot be done but by the grace of baptism.

"2. That they ought to refute and take any of the Anabaptists' and Pelagians' opinions contrary to the premises, and every other man's opinion agreeable unto the said Anabaptists' and Pelagians' opinions in this behalf, for detestable heresies, and utterly to be condemned." (Wall's Hist. Infant Bapt., vol. 1, p. 524.) But the Anabaptists replied: "That it is as lawful to christen a child in a tub of water at home, or in a ditch by the way, as in a fontstone in the church." (Fuller's Ch. Hist., vol. 2, p. 71.)

In 1538, according to Bishop Burnet, "There was a commission sent to Cranmer, Stokesley, Sampson, and some others, to enquire after Anabaptists, to proceed against them, to restore the penitent, to burn their books, to deliver the obstinate to the secular arm."

In 1539, King Henry married Lady Anne of Cleves. From that time Fuller says: "Dutchmen flocked faster than formerly to England. Many of these had active souls; so that whilst their hands were busy about their manufactures, their heads were also beating about points of

THE EPISCOPALIANS. 77

divinity. Hereof they had many rude notions, too ignorant to manage them themselves, and too proud to crave the direction of others. Their minds had a by-stream of activity more than what sufficed to drive on their vocation; and this waste of their souls they employed in needless speculations, and soon after began to broach their strange opinions, being branded with the general name of Anabaptists. These Anabaptists, for the main, are but 'Donatists new dipped;' and this year they first appeared in our English Chronicles; for I read that four Anabaptists, three men and one woman, all Dutch, bare fagots at Paul's cross, November 24th, and, three days after, a man and a woman of their sect were burned at Smithfield." (Ch. Hist., vol. 1, p. 97.)

In 1540, Parliament decreed against some who held "that infants ought not to be baptized, and if baptized, to be rebaptized when they came to years of discretion." (Collier's Eccl. Hist., vol. 5, p. 69.)

In 1542, Parliament passed the following very remarkable law: "All books likewise impugning the holy sacrament of the altar, or maintaining the damnable opinions of the Anabaptists, are prohibited under forfeiture and fines. The reading of the Bible is likewise prohibited to all under the degrees of gentlemen and gentlewomen." (Collier's Eccl. Hist., vol. 5, p. 95.)

Queen Elizabeth ordered, 1560, all Anabaptists, foreign and English, to leave the kingdom in twenty-one days, because their "misbelief gained ground" and many "were miserably misled." (Collier's Eccl. Hist., vol. 6, p. 332.)

From this period although the Baptists greatly increased yet they were bitterly persecuted. I give here the testimony of the celebrated Dr. Featley, a most violent enemy and persecutor of the Baptists. He says: "So we may say the name of the father of the Anabaptists signifyeth in English a senseless piece of wood or block, a very blockhead was he, yet out of that block were cut those chips that kindled such a fire in Germany, Halsatia, and Servia that could not be fully quenched, no, not with the blood of 150,000 of those killed in war or put to death in several places by the magistrates. This fire in the reign of Queen Elizabeth and King James and our precious sovereign till now was covered under the ashes, or if it broke out at any time, by the care of the ecclesiastical and civil magistrates it was soon put out. But of late since the unhappy distractions which our sins have brought upon us, the temporal sword being other ways employed, and the spiritual locked up in the scabbard, this sect among others hath so far presumed upon the protection of the State, that it hath held weekly conventicals, rebaptized hundreds of men and women together in the twilight in the rivulets and several arms of the Thames and elsewhere, dipping them over head and ears." (The Dippers Dipped, or the Anabaptists Plunged over Head and Ears. London, 1647. Preface, p. 3.)

The feeling of Bishop Latimer toward the Baptists was the common one. He said in a sermon before Edward VI: "The Anabaptists that were burnt here in divers towns in England went to their death even intrepid, as ye will say, without any fear in the world, cheerfully. Well, let them go."

All that could be said of these people was that they were Baptists. Hess, in his Life of Zwingle, says of them: "Their morality was rigid, their exterior simple; they disdained riches, or affected to do so; and their austere demeanor impressed the multitude with reverence, and at the same time their doctrines seduced them."

In America when they had power the Episcopalians were no better. One law passed in Virginia will give an idea of their intolerance. I quote from Henning's Statutes at Large, Laws of Virginia, vol. 2, p. 165, December 14th, 1662: "Whereas many schismatical persons out of their averseness to the orthodox established religion, or out of the new-fangled conceits of their own heretical inventions, refused to have their children baptized. Be it therefore enacted, by the authority aforesaid, that all persons that, in contempt of the divine sacrament of baptism, shall refuse when they may carry their child to a lawful minister in that county to have them baptized shall be amersed two thousand pounds of tobacco; half to the informer, half to the publique."

And these statutes were put into execution. A Baptist minister in jail in Virginia, put there by Episcopalians, was no uncommon thing.

Dr. Hawks, who was himself an Episcopalian, says of the Baptists of Virginia: "Their first preachers came from the North, and some few arose in the South: all met with opposition from those in power. 'The ministers (says Leland) were imprisoned, and the disciples buffeted.' This is but too true. No dissenters in Virginia experienced for a time harsher treatment than did the Baptists. They were beaten and imprisoned; and cruelty taxed its ingenuity to devise new modes of punishment and annoyance. The usual consequences followed; persecution made friends for its victims; and the men who were not permitted to speak in public, found willing auditors in the sympathizing crowds who gathered around the prisons to hear them preach from grated windows." (Contrib. Eccl. Hist. U. S., vol. 1, p. 121.)

With this history of persecution and bloodshed the Episcopal Church can lay no claim to open communion. We therefore justly arrive at the conclusion that the Episcopalians are close communionists. I know none who demand more at the Lord's Table. The Episcopalians do not ask, nor expect others to participate with them.

CHAPTER VII.

THE TERMS OF COMMUNION IN THE PRESBYTERIAN CHURCH. ARE THE PRESBYTERIANS CLOSE COMMUNIONISTS?

ON this communion question the declarations and acts of the Presbyterian Church have been very explicit. They have spoken in no uncertain terms. I present the facts:

1. Among Presbyterians, conversion, baptism and church membership are prerequisites to the Lord's Supper.

The Confession of Faith says: "There be only two sacraments ordained by Christ our Lord in the Gospel, that is to say, baptism and the Supper of the Lord." (Art. 27.)

This is the exact order we claim.

Calvin says in the Catechism of the Church at Geneva: "Is it enough to receive both of the sacraments once in a lifetime? It is enough so to receive baptism, which may not be repeated. It is different with the Supper. What is the difference? By baptism the Lord adopts us and brings us into his church, so as thereafter to regard us as a part of his household. After he has admitted us among the number of his people he testifies by the Supper that he takes a continual interest in nourishing us."

Henry Bullinger says: "Unto the baptism of our Lord Christ, is coupled the sacrament of the body and blood of our Lord which we call the Lord's Supper. For, those whom the Lord hath regenerated with the laver of regeneration, those doth he also feed with his spiritual food; and nourish them unto eternal life: wherefore it followeth necessarily, that we entreat next of the holy Supper of the Lord." (Sermons on the Sacraments, p. 197.)

Rev. Wm. C. Roberts, D.D., Moderator of the Presbyterian General Assembly, and Secretary of the Board of Home Missions of the Presbyterian Church of the United States, says:

NEW YORK, May 10, 1892.

REV. J. T. CHRISTIAN, Jackson, Miss.

Dear Bro.: Yours of the 4th inst. has just come to hand. The terms of admission to the Lord's Supper in the Presbyterian Church are credible evidence of conversion. We require that at the beginning of a holy life. We require baptism before one is to be publicly recognized as a church member. We do not deem church membership essential to salvation, but we hold that every converted person will necessarily desire to be identified with God's people. There are no other prerequisites to membership in the Presbyterian Church.

Hoping that the above will be satisfactory, I remain,   Yours fraternally,

WM. C. ROBERTS.

I have at hand a remarkably fine letter from Dr. Theodore Cuyler, for thirty years pastor of Lafayette Square Presbyterian Church, Brooklyn, N. Y. He says:

LAFAYETTE AVENUE PRESBYTERIAN CHURCH.
BROOKLYN, April 3, 1890.

Dear Brother: In reply to your questions I would say:

1. The terms of communion in the Presbyterian Church require a previous open confession of the Lord Jesus Christ as Saviour and Lord. That presupposes a membership in some evangelical church.

2. Baptism is an essential part of an open profession of Jesus Christ, and of reception into the visible church.

3. I do not suppose there is any difference between the Presbyterians and the Baptists in the terms of communion.

I write in haste; but allow me to express my devout gratitude for all that the great Baptist church is doing for the maintenance of sound evangelical doctrine and for the spread of the kingdom of Christ.

Yours fraternally,

THEODORE L. CUYLER.

The American *Presbyterian* says: "Open communion is an absurdity, when it means communion with the unbaptized."

Dr. Philip Schaff says: "The communion is for baptized believers, and for them only. Baptism is the sacramental sign and seal of regeneration and conversion; the Lord's Supper is the sacrament of sanctification and growth in spiritual life." (Teaching, p. 193.)

The eminent Presbyterian preacher of New Orleans, Dr. B. M. Palmer, says: "The terms of communion with us are the profession of saving faith in Christ and the public acknowledgment of this in baptism."

Dr. John Dick says: "Every person who has been baptized does not possess the moral qualifications which would entitle him to be accounted a disciple of Christ. He may be an open apostate from the faith; or he may be so ignorant of religion, and so irregular in his conduct, that it would be an abuse of charity to consider him as a Christian. Hence we demand, in candidates for the Lord's table, a competent measure of knowledge, a profession of faith in Christ, and a behaviour that will justify us in believing them to be sincere. 'All ignorant and ungodly persons,' says our church, 'as they are unfit to enjoy communion with him, so they are unworthy of the Lord's table, and cannot without great sin against Christ, while they remain such, partake of these holy mysteries, or be admitted thereunto.'" (Lect. Theol., p. 421.)

It has already been intimated, in the above, that the participant in the Lord's Supper must be a member of the church. The Confession emphasizes that the administration of the Lord's Supper is the distinctive act of a "particular church." I read: "The ordinances established by Christ, the head, *in a particular church*, which is regularly constituted with its proper officers, are prayer, singing praises, reading, expounding and preaching the Word of God; administering baptism and the Lord's Supper; public solemn fasting and thanksgiving, catechising, making collections for the poor, and other pious purposes; exercising discipline; and blessing the people." (Form of Govern., chap. vii.)

Nothing can be more evident from these statements than that the Presbyterians demand conversion, baptism and church membership before the Lord's Supper.

2. Presbyterians demand that the Supper shall be administered by a duly ordained minister. Of Baptism it is declared: "Baptism is not to be unnecessarily delayed; nor to be administered, in any case, by any private person; but by a minister of Christ, called to be steward of the mysteries of God." (Directory for Worship, chap. vii.) Of the Lord's Supper it is said: "The Lord Jesus hath in this ordinance, appointed his ministers

to declare his word of institution to the people, to pray, and bless the elements of bread and wine, and thereby to set them apart from a common to a holy use; and to take and break the bread, to take the cup, and (they communicating also themselves) to give both to the communicants; but to none who are not then present in the congregation." (Con. Faith, Art. xxix, sec. iii.) And the same thing is taught in the Larger Catechism, question 169.

Dr. A. Green, in his Lectures on the Shorter Catechism, vol. 2, p. 358, says: "It is held by us essential, that a regularly ordained minister of the gospel should administer this ordinance."

3. Presbyterians declare that the Baptists are no closer than others. This can be proved from many sources.

The New York *Observer*, the oldest Presbyterian paper in this country, says: "It is not a want of Charity which compels the Baptist to restrict his invitation. He has no hesitation in admitting the personal piety of his unimmersed brethren. Presbyterians do not invite the unbaptized, however pious they may be. It is not uncharitable. It is not bigotry on the part of the Baptists to confine their communion to those whom they consider the baptized."

The Interior, Chicago, the organ of the Western Presbyterians, says: "We agree with the Baptists in saying that unbaptized persons should not partake of the Lord's Supper. Their view compels them to think that we are not baptized, and shuts them up to close communion. Close communion is, in our judgment, a more defensible position than open communion, which is justified on the ground that baptism is not a prerequisite to the Lord's Supper. To charge Baptists with bigotry because they abide by the logical consequences of their system is absurd."

Dr. John Hunter, for thirty years pastor at Jackson, Miss., says: "I do not know that there is any special difference in the terms of admission to the communion table between Baptists and Presbyterians; that is to say that both require personal faith in an atoning Saviour, and both require communicants to be baptized."

Dr. Griffin says: "I agree with the advocates of close communion in two points: (1) that baptism is the initiating ordinance which introduces us into the visible church; of course, where there is no baptism there are no visible churches; (2) that we ought not to commune with those who are not baptized, and, of course, are not church members, even if we regard them as Christians. Should a pious Quaker so far depart from his principles as to wish to commune with me at the Lord's table, while yet he refused to be baptized, I could not receive him; because there is such a relationship established between the two ordinances that I have no right to separate them; in other words, I have no right to send the sacred elements out of the church."

Dr. John Hall, one of the greatest preachers in this country, says: "I think that all evangelical churches look for baptized persons as communicants. The Baptists differ from their brethren as to the time and mode of baptism. I do not think the Baptists and Presbyterians differ in any other respect as to the terms of communion at the Lord's table."

The Baptists are not, therefore, illiberal on account of this practice. It is conceded that we have a right to have principles, and to stand by them. This is all we have ever asked.

4. Presbyterians claim that they have a right to make such laws as they may choose to govern the approach of communicants to their table. In doing this they contend that they have not gone beyond their rights, although they should make stringent laws governing their own members. Hence I read in the Confession of Faith: "That in perfect consistency with the above principle of common right, every Christian church, or union or association of particular churches, is entitled to declare the terms of admission into its communion, and the qualifications of its ministers and members, as well as the whole system of its internal government which Christ has appointed: that in the exercise of this right, they may, notwithstanding, err, in

making the terms of communion either too lax or too narrow: yet, even in this case, they do not infringe upon the liberty, or the rights of others, but only make an improper use of their own." (Con. Faith, Form Govern., B. I, sec. 2.)

These Church Rights were fully endorsed by the General Assembly in 1839. That body said: "Every Christian church, or association of churches, is entitled to declare the terms of admission into its communion."

The Presbyterians not only assumed that they had a right to make such laws, but they made them and carried them into execution. On October the 20th, 1645, the Presbyterians in the English Parliament passed a very full and exclusive law on this subject. It was known as: "An ordinance of the Lords and Commons assembled in Parliament about Suspension from the Lord's Supper." (Rushwood, vol. 6, pp. 210–212.) That law resulted in the XXXth Article of the Confession of Faith, which is the law of the Presbyterian Church to-day. That Article reads in sections iii and iv: "Church censures are necessary for the reclaiming and gaining of offending brethren; for deterring of others from like offenses; for purging out of that leaven which might infect the whole lump; for vindicating the honour of Christ, and the holy profession of the Gospel; and for preventing the wrath of God, which might justly fall upon the church, if they should suffer this covenant, and the seals thereof, to be profaned by notorious and obstinate offenders.

"For the better attaining of these ends, the officers of the church are to proceed by admonition, suspension from the sacrament of the Lord's Supper for a season, and by excommunication from the church, according to the nature of the crime, and demerit of the person."

The Larger Catechism, Q. 173, is in full accord with the above article. It reads: "May any who profess the faith, and desire to come to the Lord's Supper, be kept from it? Such as are found to be ignorant or scandalous, notwithstanding their profession of the faith and desire to come to the Lord's Supper, may and ought to be kept from that sacrament by the power which Christ has left in his church, until they receive instruction and manifest their reformation."

And for fear that somebody might not consider the Confession of Faith a close communion document it is put down under the Directory of Worship, chapter VIII:

"I. The communion, or supper of the Lord, is to be celebrated frequently; but how often, may be determined by the minister and eldership of each congregation, as they may judge most for edification.

"II. The ignorant and scandalous are not to be admitted to the Lord's Supper.

"III. It is proper that public notice should be given to the congregation, at least, the Sabbath before the administration of this ordinance, and that, either then, or on some day of the week, the people be instructed in its nature, and due preparation for it; that all may come in a suitable manner to this holy feast."

Dr. A. A. Hodge sums up the entire matter in these words: "All church power must be exercised in an orderly manner through the officers spoken of above, freely chosen for this purpose by the brethren; and it relates: 1. To matters of doctrine. She has a right to set forth a public declaration of the truths which she believes, and which are to be acknowledged by all who enter her communion. That is, she has a right to frame creeds or confessions of faith, as her testimony for the truth and her protest against error. And as she has been commissioned to teach all nations, she has the right of selecting teachers, of judging of their fitness, of ordaining and sending them forth in the field, and of recalling and deposing them when unfaithful. 2. The Church has power to set down rules for the ordering of public worship. 3. She has power to make rules for her own government; such as every church has in its book of discipline, etc. 4. She has power to receive into fellowship, and to exclude the unworthy from her own communion." (Com. on Con. Faith, pp. 501, 502.)

The conclusion is inevitable, that if Presbyterians have laid down such stringent rules in the observance of the Supper, and claim that they have a full right so to do, they cannot consistently object to any practice that may exist among the Baptists.

5. The history of the Presbyterian Church has been one of strict communion. A study of their history developed the fact that they have not sought communion with other denominations; nor has there been inter-communion among the various Presbyterian bodies. I invite your attention to the practice of the Presbyterians in a number of countries.

The Presbyterians originated in Switzerland with John Calvin. He was by no means an open communionist. So far from this being the case he instituted the most rigid laws against others; and even put Servetus to death because he was not in sympathy with his views. The celebrated Francis Turretin, Professor of Theology in Geneva, shows the spirit of that country toward others. He says: "Since magistrates are keepers of both tables, and the care of religion pertains to them, they ought to provide that it should suffer no injury, and should in wisdom oppose those who assert it, lest the poison insinuate itself more widely, and be diffused through the whole body. But magistrates cannot protect religion, unless they restrain the obstinate and factious contemners thereof. Such interference, both the glory of God, of which they are the defenders, and the safety of the commonwealth, of which they are the guardians, demand. If less evils are restrained by heavy penalties, this, which is the greatest, which injures the trust of God, which blasphemes his name, which rends the Church, which corrupts the faith, and brings into danger the safety of the faithful, should not be permitted to go unpunished. Rather is there frequently required, that a speedy and powerful remedy be applied; inasmuch, as from this quarter, the destruction of the whole body is threatened, unless the application be quickly made." (De Polit. Ecc. gubern., Tim. iii, Loc. xviii, quaesti xxxiv, p. 278.)

In Scotland it was required: "That all kings and princes, at their coronation, and reception of their princely authority, shall make their faithful promise, by their solemn oath, in the presence of their eternal God, that during the whole of their lives, they shall serve the same eternal God, to the utmost of their power, according as he hath required in his most holy word, contained in the Old and New Testament; and, according to the same word, shall maintain the true religion of Christ Jesus, the preaching of his holy word, the due and rightful administration of the sacraments now received and preached within this realm, (according to the

Confession of Faith immediately preceding) and shall abolish and gainstand all false religion contrary to the same; and shall rule the people committed to their charge, according to the will and command of God, revealed in his foresaid word, and according to the laudable laws and constitutions received in this realm, no wise repugnant to the said will of the eternal God; and shall procure to the utmost of their power, to the kirk of God, and the whole Christian people, true and perfect peace in all time coming; and that they shall be careful to root out of their empire all heretics and enemies to the true worship of God, who shall be convicted by the true kirk of God of the aforesaid crimes." (Coronation Oath in the National Covenant.)

In Scotland there was a general form of expulsion of unworthy persons from the Lord's table, in connection with the ministration of the sacrament. This was called excommunication or "fencing the tables." (Fisher's Ch. Hist., p. 368.) It was further required that office holders should be communicants in the Presbyterian Church.

The first Confession of Helvetia declares: "Seeing that every magistrate is of God, his chief duty, except it please him to exercise tyranny, consists in this: to defend religion from all blasphemy, to promote it, as the prophet teaches, out of the word of God, to see it put in practice, as far as it lies in him." The latter

Confession, which was expressly approved by the Church of Scotland and other Presbyterians, says: "Magistracy, of whatever sort it be, is ordained of God himself, for the peace and tranquility of mankind; so that the magistracy ought to have the chief place in the world. If he be an adversary of the Church, he may greatly hinder and disturb it; but if he be a friend and member of the Church, he is a most profitable member, and may excellently aid and advance it. His principal duty is to procure and maintain peace and public tranquility; which doubtless he will never do more happily than when he is seasoned with the fear of God, and true religion, particularly when we shall, after the examples of the most holy kings and princes of the people of the Lord, advance the preaching of the truth, and the pure unadulterated faith, shall extirpate falsehood, and all superstition, impiety and idolatry, and shall defend the Church of God; for indeed we teach that the care of religion doth chiefly appertain to the holy magistrate."

The Confession of Saxony says: "The word of God doth in general, teach this, concerning the power of the magistrate; first, that God wills that the magistrates, without all doubt, should sound forth the voice of the moral law among men, according to the ten commandments, or law natural, by-laws forbidding idolatry and blasphemies, as well as murders, theft, etc., for well it has been said of old: "The magistrate is a keeper of the law, i. e., of the first and second table, as concerning discipline and good order. This ought to be their special care (of kingdoms and of their rulers), to hear and embrace the true doctrine of the Son of God, and to cherish the churches, according to Ps. ii and xxiv, and Isaiah xlix, and kings and queens shall be thy nurses, i. e., let commonwealths be nurses of the church, and to godly studies."

The Dutch Confession says: God "hath armed the magistrate with a sword, to punish the bad and to defend the good. Furthermore, it is their duty to be careful not only to preserve the civil polity, but also to endeavor that the ministry be preserved: that all idolatry and counterfeit worship be abolished, the kingdom of Antichrist be brought down, and the kingdom of Christ be enlarged; in fine, that it is their duty to bring it to pass, that the holy word of the Gospel be preached everywhere, that all men may serve God, purely and freely, according to the prescribed will of his word."

The French Confession says: "God hath delivered the sword unto the magistrate's hand, that sins committed against both tables of God's law, not only against the second, but the first also, may be suppressed."

There is nothing of open communion in these Presbyterian laws and Confessions of Faith.

When we recollect that these heretics and blasphemers were none other than Baptists, and that the magistrates were to root them out, and either banish them from the country or burn them at the stake, we shudder. These things settle beyond a doubt that the Presbyterians of Europe were not open communionists.

In the United States the history of Presbyterianism is against open communion. I present a statement from Thomas Jefferson on Presbyterianism. He says: "The atmosphere of our country is unquestionably charged with a threatening cloud of fanaticism, lighter in some parts, denser in others, but too heavy in all. I had no idea, however, that in Pennsylvania, the cradle of toleration, and freedom of religion, it could have risen to the height you describe. This must be owing to the growth of Presbyterianism. Here Episcopalian and Presbyterian, Methodist and Baptist, join together in hymning their Maker, listen with attention and devotion to each others' preachers, and all mix in society with perfect harmony. It is not so in the districts where Presbyterianism prevails undividedly. Their ambition and tyranny would tolerate no rival, if they had power. Systematical at grasping at an ascendency over all other sects, they aim at engrossing the education of the country, they are hostile to every institution that they do not direct; are jealous of seeing others begin to attend at all to that object." (Works, vol. 4, p. 358.)

On the same subject he says in his letter to William Short: "The Presbyterian clergy are the loudest, the most intolerant of all sects; the most tyrannical and ambitious; ready at the word of the lawgiver, if such a word could now be obtained, to put the torch to the pile, and to rekindle in this virgin hemisphere the flames in which their oracle, Calvin, consumed the poor Servetus, because he could not subscribe to the proposition of Calvin, that magistrates have a right to exterminate all heretics to the Calvinistic creed. They pant to re-establish, by law, that holy inquisition, which they can now only infuse into public opinion." (p. 322.)

When the great struggle came in Virginia for the complete disestablishment of the Episcopal Church the Presbyterians passed many noble resolutions. But when, at length, the General Assembly passed a law, that "a general assessment for the support of religion ought to be extended to those who profess the public worship of the Deity," and there was a chance for the Presbyterians to receive State aid, they faltered. (Journal House of Delegates, October, 1784, 32.) Rives says this was "in a memorial presented by the united clergy of the Presbyterian Church." (Life and Times of Madison, vol. 1, p. 601.)

Dr. Foot, a Presbyterian historian of Virginia,

says that the Hanover Presbytery prepared for the Legislature, November 12th, 1784, a plan of assessment as follows:

"1. Religion as a spiritual system is not to be considered as an object of human legislation, but may be in a civil view, as preserving the existence and promoting the happiness of society. 2. That public worship and public periodical instruction to the people, be maintained in this view by a general assessment for this purpose. 3. That every man, as a good citizen, be obliged to declare himself attached to some religious community, publicly known to profess the belief of one God, His righteous providence, our accountableness to Him, and a future state of rewards and punishments. 4. That every citizen should have liberty annually to direct his assessed proportion to such community as he chooses. 5. Provides that twelve tithables shall exclusively direct the application of the money contributed for their support." (Sketches of Virginia, p. 338.)

President Madison, writing of this struggle, under date of April 12th, 1785, says of this proposal to continue taxation: "The Episcopal people are generally for it—the tax. The Presbyterians seem as ready to set up an establishment which is to take them in, as they were to pull down that which shut them out. I do not know a more shameful contrast than might be found between their memorials on the latter and the former occasions." (Rive's Life Madison, vol. 1, p. 630.)

Referring to the Presbyterians in this crisis Dr. Hawks says: "When that great end (the giving a death blow to the legalized superiority) was once obtained, and every religious society stood upon the same level, the question in dispute assumed to these allies a very different aspect, and they deserted the standard under which they had before achieved their victory. They had prostrated the church; they had proved themselves not at all reluctant to strip her clergy of that competent maintenance which was secured to them by the possession of property; but they now manifested an aversion, more rational than consistent, in being left to find a precarious support for themselves, in the tender mercies of a set of voluntary contributors." (Hawks' Hist. Prot. Epis. Ch., pp. 151, 152.)

In every country where Presbyterians have had power they have persecuted.

I do not regard the people who are Presbyterians as worse than others; but the trouble is in the organic law of Presbyterianism. Perhaps Dr. Guthrie has rightly put it: "So I fear that, on departing from the Church of Rome, we carried into our Protestantism—as was not unnatural—some of her ancient superstitions; just as our fathers carried into their practices some of her *intolerant principles*. We cannot approve of their intolerance, yet it admits of an apology. THEY HAD BEEN SUCKLED BY THE WOLF, and it is no great wonder that, WITH THE MILK OF THE WOLF, THEY SHOULD HAVE IMBIBED SOME OF HER NATURE." (Gospel in Ezek., p. 213.)

The Presbyterian Churches of this country do not commune with their European brethren. Dr. Breckinridge, in his debate with Archbishop Hughes of the Catholic Church, says: "Mr. Hughes says: And if they have changed, as he asserts, let the next General Assembly break communion with their sister Presbyteries in Europe, in whose Confessions of Faith the principles of intolerance are avowed as a doctrine. Now the truth is, Mr. Hughes, ignorantly I would fain hope, has entirely falsified the facts. We hold no such communion with any such churches. The Church of Scotland has an establishment, and retains the intolerant doctrine. The consequence is we have no communion with her. The Irish Church (the Synod of Ulster) receives the regium donum. We have no reciprocity with her." (Hughes and Breckinridge Debate, p. 527.)

We have a more recent example. The Pan-Presbyterian Council at Philadelphia, in 1880, refused to observe the Lord's Supper together, upon the ground that the Supper is a Church ordinance, to be observed only by those who are amenable to the discipline of the body, and therefore not to be observed by separate Church organizations acting together. Substantially upon this ground the Old School General Assembly long before, being invited to unite at the Lord's table with the New School body with whom they had dissolved ecclesiastical relations declined to do so. (See Strong's Systemat. Theol., p. 549.)

Dr. Engles, editor of the Philadelphia *Presbyterian*, September 12th, 1840, took the ground that the Old School Presbyterians could not commune with the Methodists and the New School Presbyterians. In reply to some resolutions of the West Hanover Presbytery, Virginia, formally condemning this doctrine, he observes: "As Presbyterians we profess to receive our denominational distinction from the symbols of faith which we adopt; and we regard other denominations as having their distinctive belief and character, of which we judge by their public symbols. The opinion that Confessions or doctrinal formularies are only obligatory on the ministry, and not on the people of a church, is, in our judgment, a most dangerous one; the adoption of it must at once destroy the homogeneity of a church, and give full license to the people to embrace every form of error. On the contrary, it is presumed that a Presbyterian believes in Presbyterian doctrine, or why is he a Presbyterian? And that a Methodist believes in the doctrines of his own church, or why is he not something else? The Methodists and Presbyterians alike believe that they have very good reasons for being as they are; nay, so potent are those reasons regarded to be, that neither imagines he could ever be induced to change his position. Now all we have contended for is consistency in carrying this principle out into practice.

"As our Methodist brethren * * * have taken umbrage at our language, let us ask them if they are prepared to advise their people, on all favorable occasions, to go and commune with the Presbyterians? Do they wish them to think there is no difference between the denominations? Do they regard the difference as so trivial as to invite entire oblivion of them by their flocks, when they stray into Presbyterian folds? We judge not. Why then should they be angry with us for following their example? Holding the faith we do * * * can we, or ought we to say to the sheep of our fold—Yonder are pastures in which we believe there are poisonous weeds growing, but still there can be but little danger of occasionally feeding there? In this matter we have never found our Methodist brethren a particle more liberal than ourselves. We have never found them backward in decrying Presbyterianism; and we, on the other hand, candidly tell them, as we have often told them before, that we consider their system as very erroneous. For each of us thus to think is our right, in the exercise of Christian liberty, but is it quite possible that we should forget this, and lay aside our strong feelings on the subject, while we commune together?"

Of the New School Presbyterians Dr. Engles says: "The West Hanover resolutions express as much solicitude to be on as good terms with the New School as with the Methodists. If we understand them, they wish the whole world to know that they distinctly disavow the exclusiveness which would refuse to commune with the men whom they, as Presbyterians, helped out of the Church. If we mistake not they took an honorable part in the exclusive measures by which the New School lost their statutes in our church; we say, their statutes in our church, for although the exclusion in question did not affect their ecclesiastical organization, all the world knows that the excluded party are not now, and never have been since the passage of the acts, in the communion of the Presbyterian church. When, therefore, this Presbytery publicly says that they wish, with all 'liberality and Christian courtesy,' to hold communion with them—what must they think? If such language does not sound like a bitter mockery in their ears, we are not well skilled in sounds. The measure by which the New School was excluded from the Presbyterian church was either righteous or unrighteous; if the former, why should we make any professions of attachment which our actions do not sustain, or if the latter, why do we not magnanimously avow it, and invite them back in a body? We believe it was righteous, and whether right or wrong in our belief, we contend that, while the causes exist which led to it, it is utterly inexpedient to hold communion with those churches." (Philadelphia *Presbyterian*, September 12th, 1840.)

From the Synodical proceedings of one of the Valley States we read: The Committee on Bills and Overtures, to whom was referred the question: "Is it proper that there should be intercommunion between Presbyterians and those denominations who hold Arminian sentiments?" presented the following report which was adopted: "That after giving it all the attention which the importance of the subject demands, they are of the opinion that for Presbyterians to hold communion in sealing ordinances with those who deny the doctrines of grace, through the blood of Christ, etc., is highly prejudicial to the truth as it is in Jesus. Nor can such intercommunion answer any valuable purpose to those who practice it, as two cannot walk together unless they be agreed. Yet, as there are persons who have received distorted views of the doctrines of grace, who notwithstanding admit these doctrines in fact, although they are prejudiced against the terms generally used in the discussion of these subjects, your committee are of the opinion that, if such manifest a desire to hold communion with us, that, after being conversed with, and having received satisfaction on these and other points on which their church and ours disagree, and having obtained satisfactory evidence of their piety, charity requires that they should be admitted to occasional intercommunion." (Union Evangelist, and Presbyterian Advocate, 1820, vol. 2, pp. 96-99.)

And from the proceeding of one other Synod we read: "The committee are of the opinion that for Presbyterians to hold communion in sealing ordinances with those who belong to churches holding doctrines contrary to our standards, is incompatible with the purity and the peace of our church, and highly prejudicial to the truth as it is in Jesus. Nor can such communion answer any valuable purpose, etc. In accordance with these views, your committee are of opinion that the practice of inviting to the communion all who are in good standing in their own churches, is calculated to do much evil, and should not be continued, while every church session is, however, left at liberty to admit to occasional communion members of other denominations, after having conversed with them, and received satisfaction of their soundness in the faith, and Christian practice." (Extracts from Synodical Records, 1832, ut supra, vol. 3, p. 240.)

We are certain, therefore, that open communion among Presbyterians is of recent origin, and contrary to the well known history of Presbyterianism. So much so that Dr. David Montfort says: "As to how far catholic or open communion has been practiced, I am not very accurately informed. The language of the divines of Westminster afford no evidence to me that it was sustained by them. It is very certain that four different denominations subscribing this same confession of faith, and adhering most tenaciously to it, discountenanced the practice altogether. I am exceeding happy to be informed that in the Synod of Pittsburg, where in our great struggle, Presbyterianism prevailed in its greatest purity, it is not generally practiced. The practice is of recent date. My own recollection, and the testimony of older men, assure me that the practice of our forefathers was exceedingly strict. That it was rarely, if at all, the case with them for their own members to commune out of the particular church to which they belonged. That a sojourner was not admitted except on a certificate of his good standing in his own church. So far were our forefathers from the present practice of laxness in this day."

From the above history Presbyterians can hardly censure the Baptists for being close communionists. We have no close communion record like this. It cannot be denied that Presbyterians concede all we claim as to the terms of communion, and further declare that we are consistent in our practice.

CHAPTER VIII.

THE TERMS OF COMMUNION IN THE CONGREGATIONAL CHURCH. ARE THE CONGREGATIONALISTS CLOSE COMMUNIONISTS?

I PRESENT the testimony that the Congregationalists have the same terms of approach to the Lord's table as have the Baptists.

The Congregationalists require conversion, baptism, church membership as prerequisites to the Lord's Supper. This we learn from various sources.

Dr. Henry M. Dexter says: "Only members in good standing in the visible church, have a right to partake of the Lord's Supper." (Congregationalism, p. 163.)

George P. Fisher, D.D., Professor of Ecclesiastical History in Yale University, says: "After the rite of baptism had been administered, they gathered in an assembly for common prayer. Then they saluted one another with a kiss; and the service concluded with the administration of the communion, prayers and thanksgiving, to which the congregation responded 'amen,' forming a part of the service." (Begin. Christ., p. 566.)

Dr. Dwight, President of Yale College, says: "It is an indispensable qualification for this ordinance that the candidate for communion be a member of the visible church in full standing. By this I intend that he should be a man of piety; that he should have made a public profession of religion, and that he should have been baptized." (Syst. Theol., Ser. 160, B. 8, ch. 4, sec. 7, vol. 4, pp. 365, 366.)

The Independent, one of the most widely circulated, and perhaps the most influential Pedobaptist paper in the country, in an editorial, says: "Leading writers of all denominations declare that converts must be baptized before they can be invited to the communion table. This is the position generally taken. But Baptists regarding sprinkling a nullity—no baptism at all—look upon Presbyterians, Methodists, and others, as unbaptized persons." "The other churches cannot urge the Baptists to become open communionists till they themselves take the position that all who love our Lord Jesus Christ, the unbaptized as well as the baptized, may be invited to the communion table." (Editorial, July, 1879.)

These authorities prove beyond a doubt that Congregationalists demand of communicants the same qualifications as do the Baptists.

The Congregationalists teach that Pedobaptists are close communionists, and that the Baptists are consistent in their practice.

The Congregationalist, the organ of the New England Congregational Churches, says: "Congregationalists have uniformly, until here and there an exception has arisen of late years, required baptism and church membership as the prerequisite of a seat at the table of the Lord. It is a part of the false 'liberality' which now prevails in certain quarters, to welcome 'everybody who thinks he loves Christ' to commune in his body and blood. Such a course is a first step in breaking down that distinction between the church and the world, which our Saviour emphasized; and it seems to us it is an unwise and mistaken act for which no Scripture warrant exists." (Editorial, July 9th, 1879.)

Rev. G. W. Wright says: "The intelligent consistent defence of close communion on the part of the Baptists does not proceed on the supposition that immersed persons are the only regenerated believers; but they base their refusal to invite unbaptized persons to the Lord's table on the same grounds of order and expediency on which other denominations refuse to invite unbaptized persons to commune with them." (Bibliotheca Sacra for 1874.)

The Independent says: "We have never been disposed to charge the Baptist churches with any special narrowness or bigotry in their rule of admission to the Lord's table. We do not see how it differs from that commonly admitted and established among Presbyterian churches."

Said Henry Ward Beecher, in the *Christian*

Union: "A Pedobaptist, who believes that baptism is prerequisite to communion, has no right to censure the Baptist churches for close communion. On this question, there is a great deal of pulling out of motes by people whose own vision is not clear." In another issue of the same paper he says: "We have no disposition to join in the censure which is so freely bestowed upon Baptists for their principle and practice of restricted communion. Their course on this question, however mistaken, is certainly consistent, and we must yield them the respect due to all who adhere firmly to their conscientious convictions."

The Advance, of Chicago, in an editorial, November 10th, 1868, says: "As to the question of invitation to the Lord's table, while sympathizing with much that is urged in favor of separating that ordinance from church membership, and throwing it open to all upon their individual responsibility after due warning, we have not yet seen our way clear to adopt that view. Neither New Testament practice, nor a wise regard to the effect, appear to us to favor such a method. The mode of the institution of the Lord's Supper, the apostolic explanations and instructions, and the primitive practice, agree in presenting it as an ordinance of the church distinctively—standing as one of the two sacraments which mark and bless the professed disciples of Christ.

Besides, the idea of each participant coming as an individual soul, upon his own responsibility merely, robs the ordinance of its distinctive organic meaning as a supper—that is, a joint meal of the members of a family, and not the catching up of a morsel by hungry strangers who compose a chance crowd."

Listen again to the testimony of an eminent Congregationalist, Rev. Dr. Woolcot Caulkins, in the *Andover Review:* "It has never been denied that the Puritan way of maintaining the purity and doctrinal soundness of the churches is to secure a soundly converted membership. There is one denomination of Puritans which has never deviated a hair's breadth from this way. The Baptists have always insisted that regenerate persons only ought to receive the sacraments of the church. And they have depended absolutely upon this provision for the purity and doctrinal soundness of their churches. They are strictly Congregational in polity. But they have never imposed a creed test for membership. It is true that they have adopted in general confessions various standards—a recension of the Westminster Confession (Philadelphia, 1742), and the New Hampshire Confession (1833), and some churches have confessions of their own. But they expressly repudiate the imposition of any formal creed upon any church or upon any member."

To the question whether Baptists have failed

to maintain sound doctrine, Dr. Caulkins replies by quoting the words of Dr. J. L. Withrow, Presbyterian, Boston: "I suppose there is not a denomination—I speak in no fulsome praise, but literally—I think there is not a denomination of Evangelical Christians that is throughout as sound theologically as the Baptist denomination. I believe it. After carefully considering it, I believe I speak the truth. Sound as my own denomination is, sound as some others are, and I do not cast unfriendly reflections upon any particular denomination, I do say, in my humble judgment, there is not an Evangelical denomination in America to-day that is as true to the simple, plain Gospel of God, as it is recorded in the Word, as the Baptist denomination."

High praise, this.

The practice of Congregationalists has been against open communion. They passed in America the most stringent laws against other denominations. They had scarcely landed in New England until they were burning witches, whipping and banishing Baptists. In 1644, the General Court of Massachusetts passed an act in which it was said: "Forasmuch as experience hath plentifully shown and often proven that since the rising of the Anabaptists, about one hundred years since, they have been the incendiaries of the commonwealths, and the infectors of persons in matters of religion, and the troublers of churches in all places where they have been, and that they who have held that the baptizing of infants unlawful, have usually held other errors or heresies, together with, though they have concealed the same till they have spied out a fit advantage and opportunity to vent them by way of scruple or question * * * it is ordered and agreed that, if any person or persons, within this jurisdiction, shall either openly condemn or oppose the baptizing of infants, or go about secretly to induce others from approbation or use thereof * * * every such person shall be sentenced to banishment."

This punishment was visited upon many. "Baptists," says Fisher, who is himself a Congregationalist, "were stigmatized as 'schismatical persons, filled with the new-fangled conceits of their heredical inventions.'" (Fisher's Church Hist., p. 476.) So late as 1679 there was a law passed against Baptists being permitted to build houses of worship. And when the First Baptist Church of Boston erected a house a Synod met the following September and gave it as its opinion that "the cause of the judgments of God upon the land was the allowing of those Baptists to worship by themselves;" therefore their meeting house was nailed up, by order of the court, in March, 1680, and Dr. Increase Mather published a book in which he said that "Antipedobaptism was a blasted error."

At the period of the Revolutionary War Dr. George P. Fisher says: "In places where no congregations had been gathered by dissidents from the prevailing system, individuals, whatever their religious belief might be, were compelled to contribute to the support of the Congregational worship there existing. This requirement was more and more counted a hardship. It is believed that in all of the colonies there were religious tests in some form. Even in Pennsylvania and Delaware, none could vote save those who professed faith in Christ. When the revolutionary contest began, it was natural that there should spring up movements to abolish the religious inequalities which were a heritage from the past. The Baptists, who were outnumbered by none of the religious bodies except the Congregationalists, and who had felt themselves especially aggrieved, at once bestirred themselves in Massachusetts and Virginia to secure the repeal of obnoxious restrictions." (Church Hist., pp. 559, 560.)

Those who settled New York were as rigid in their opinions as their New England brethren. "In 1656 it was ordained that all parishes should be forbidden to hold conventicles not in harmony with the established religion as set forth by the Synod of Dort. Fines were imposed on every preacher who broke this law, and on every one

who should attend a meeting thus prohibited."
(See Fisher's Ch. Hist., p. 477.)

With a history as intolerant as this, Puritanism, or as it was afterwards called Congregationalism, could hardly say anything against Baptist Close Communion. We never banished any one, we have never unchristianized any one, all we have asked is that we shall quietly, in the fear of God, be allowed to regulate our own affairs.

CHAPTER IX.

THE TERMS OF COMMUNION IN THE METHODIST CHURCH. ARE THE METHODISTS CLOSE COMMUNIONISTS? THE WESLEYS AND DR. COKE.

THE Methodist Church, in the same manner as the Baptists, requires baptism as a prerequisite to the Lord's Supper. The Methodist Discipline, Article 16, lays down the order upon which I have been insisting: "There are two sacraments ordained of Christ our Lord in the gospel; that is to say, Baptism and the Supper of the Lord."

Dr. Hibbard says: "It is certain that baptism is enjoined as the first public duty after discipleship; or, it may be regarded as the very act itself, or process, of visible discipleship. The very position, therefore, that baptism is made to occupy, in a relation to a course of Christian duty, viz., at the commencement, sufficiently establishes the conclusion that the ordinance of the supper, and all other observances which have an exclusive reference to the Christian profession, must come in as subsequent duties." (Hibbard on Baptism, pp. 176, 177.)

Dr. Adam Clarke says: "As no person could

partake of the paschal lamb before he was circumcised (Ex. 12:43-48), so, among the early followers of God, no person was permitted to come to the eucharist till he had been baptized." (Works, vol. 3, pp. 149, 150.)

Dr. Bennett in his recent able work on Archæology makes a similar statement. His work is edited and endorsed by two other able Methodists, one of whom is a bishop—George R. Crooks and Bishop John M. Hurst. Here is the combined authority of three of the foremost men in that denomination in this country. It is further stated that the theology of the volume is in "harmony with the doctrinal standards of the Methodist Episcopal Church." Dr. Bennett says: "None but the believers or the baptized are admitted to the meal—to feast on the flesh and blood of Jesus who was made flesh." (Archæology, p. 419.)

The history of the Methodist Church is one of close communion. There are no people more rigid in their requirements. If the Discipline is enforced, I know no one except a Methodist who can approach their table. Perhaps the facts I here present from their foremost bishops, writers and scholars will surprise you.

The entire Wesley family were violently opposed to all dissenters from the established Church of England. They could not tolerate Baptists and Presbyterians, and indeed did not fellowship any outside of the Episcopal Church. Herbert S. Skeats says of the father of Mr. John Wesley: "His father had not only conformed to the church, but was one of the most bitter, unscrupulous, and malignant opponents of dissent." (History Free Churches of England, p. 24.)

John Wesley was violent in his opposition to others. He says very plainly that baptism precedes communion. In a sermon which he preached upon, "Do this in remembrance of me," he laid down baptism as a prerequisite to communion. (Wesley's Sermons, vol. 4, p. 153.) In his Journal, vol. 1, p. 188, he says: "In the ancient church every one who was baptized communicated daily." No Baptist ever insisted upon this doctrine more strongly than did Mr. Wesley.

In practice Mr. Wesley was as strict as any high-churchman in the land. Communicating upon a letter received from one J. M. Bolzins, he says: "And yet this very man, when I was in Savannah, did I refuse to admit to the Lord's table, because he was not baptized by a minister who had been episcopally ordained. Can any one carry high-church zeal farther than this?" (Journal, vol. 1, p. 466.) I should not only say that the door was closed, but locked and barred.

Wesley wrote his brother-in-law, Wesley Hall, in 1745: "We believe it would not be right for us to administer either baptism or the Lord's Supper, unless we had a commission so to do from those bishops whom we apprehend to be in a succession from the apostles." (Tyerman's Life and Times of Wesley, vol. 1, p. 496.)

Here is another specimen of close communion. It occurred in Norwich, England, April 1st, 1759. Mr. Wesley says: "I met all at six, requiring every one to show his ticket when he came in; a thing they never had heard of before. I likewise insisted on another strange regulation; that the men and women should sit apart. A third was made the same day. It had been a custom ever since the tabernacle was built, to have the galleries full of spectators while the Lord's Supper was administered, This I judged highly improper and therefore ordered none to be admitted, but those who desired to communicate." (Journal, vol. 2, p. 17.)

About this time Mr. Wesley rebaptized five Presbyterians, and called their baptism lay baptism, because they had not been *episcopally ordained*. I will let Bishop McTyeire recite this interesting occurrance. Says the Bishop: "Incredible as it may seem, John Wesley, in that very church, a few days afterward solemnly and rather demonstratively rebaptized five Presbyterians, who had received *lay baptism* in their infancy—that is, in the jargon of apostolic succession, they had been baptized by Dissenting ministers—*possibly* by his own grandfather, Dr.

Annesley. Charles, about the same time, gave *episcopal* baptism to a woman who was dissatisfied with her *lay* baptism; denominating the ordinance 'hypothetical baptism'—that is, Christian baptism, provided the former administration of the ordinance by a Dissenting minister were not in accordance with the mind of God." (McTyeire's Hist. Method., pp. 147, 148.)

That ought to be close enough to satisfy our Presbyterian brethren.

I read in Tyerman's *Oxford Methodists*, preface, page vi: "Even in Georgia, Wesley excluded Dissenters from the holy communion, on 'the ground that they had not been properly baptized, and he would himself baptize only by immersion, unless the child or person was in a weak state of health."

Skeats gives a somewhat somber account of this memorable trip of Mr. Wesley to Georgia. He says: "He went there with a noble and self-sacrificing purpose, but with all of the ecclesiastical tendencies of a High Churchman, combined with a somewhat superstitious faith in what may be described as Christian magic. Instances of the latter may be found in the whole of his journals. The first occurs in his voyage to Georgia. A woman who thought she was dying, wished to receive the communion. 'At the hour of receiving,' says Wesley, 'she began to recover, and in a few days was entirely out of danger.' One of his first acts of ministerial duty in Georgia was to baptize an infant. 'The child was ill,' remarks Wesley, 'then, but recovered from that hour.' His visit to America was a failure, and his rigid and priestly adherence to the rubrics of the Established Church, which brought upon him a law-suit, ultimately compelled his return to England." (Hist. Free Churches of Eng., pp. 252, 253.)

In fact, so severe was Mr. Wesley that he was accused of being a papist. Southey, who wrote a standard life of Wesley, says: "He was accused of making his sermons so many satires upon particular persons, and for this cause his auditors fell off; for, though one might have been very well pleased to hear the others preached. at, no person liked the chance of being made the mark himself. All the quarrels which had occurred since his arrival were occasioned, it was affirmed, by his intermeddling conduct. 'Beside,' said a plain speaker, to him, 'the people say they are Protestants; but as for you, they cannot tell what religion you are of: they never heard of such religion before, and they do not know what to make of it.'" (Southey's Life of Wesley, vol. 1, p. 115.) In fact, "he was looked upon," says Tyerman, "as a Roman Catholic—(1) Because he rigidly excluded all Dissenters from the holy communion, until they first gave up their faith and principles, and, like Richard

Turner and his sons, submitted to be rebaptized by him; (2) Because Roman Catholics were received by him as saints; (3) Because he endeavored to establish and enforce confession, penance, and mortification; mixed wine with water at the sacrament; and appointed deaconesses in accordance with what he called the Apostolic Constitutions. He was in fact, a Puseyite, an hundred years before Dr. Pusey was born." (Life of Wesley, vol. 1, pp. 147, 148.) And Wesley confessed that for ten years he was a papist and knew it not.

Of the Oxford Methodists the late Bishop McTyeire, of the Southern Methodist Church, says: "He maintained the doctrine of apostolic succession, and believed no one had authority to administer the sacraments who was not *episcopally* ordained. He religiously observed saint-days and holidays, and excluded Dissenters from the holy communion, on the ground that they had not been properly baptized. He observed ecclesiastical discipline to the minutest points, and was scrupulously strict in practicing rubrics and canons * * * Sacramentarian, ritualist, legalist: What lack I yet?" (Hist. Methodism, p. 62.)

Bishop McTyeire sums Wesley up as a close communionist of the strictest character. Methodists do not get open communion from Mr. Wesley. Says the Bishop: "Following a primitive but obsolete rubric, he would baptize children only by immersion; nor could he be induced to depart from this mode unless the parents would certify that the child was weakly. Persons were not allowed to act as sponsors who were not communicants. No baptism was recognized as valid unless performed by a minister episcopally ordained; and those who had allowed their children to be baptized in any other manner were earnestly exhorted to have them rebaptized. His rigor extended even so far as to refuse the Lord's Supper to one of the most devout men of the settlement, who had not been baptized by an episcopally ordained minister; and the burial service itself was denied to such as died with what he deemed unorthodox baptism." (Hist. Method., p. 90.)

The Baptists never did require as much as is here demanded. Mr. Wesley demanded baptism, even insisted that communicants must be baptized by a minister episcopally ordained. He excluded from his table all Dissenters, that is to say Baptists, Presbyterians, and others, would not permit spectators, and required a ticket for admission. "Can any one carry high-church zeal farther than this?"

Charles Wesley was even more violent in his feelings than was John Wesley. He wrote to one of his best friends that he would rather see him "smiling in his coffin" than to see him a dissenting (or Presbyterian) preacher. Bishop McTyeire says: "His high-church feelings could hardly endure the innovation of lay preaching; but the administration of the sacraments by men not episcopally ordained was quite out of the question; it would make Dissenters out of them *ipso facto*, and bring on separation. He wrote to John Nelson: 'John, I love thee from my heart; yet, rather than see thee a Dissenting minister, I wish to see thee smiling in thy coffin.' * * * Yet this good man—this primitive Methodist—was so wedded to the Established Church that unless John Nelson, and others like him, could be 'episcopally ordained' he would rather see John 'smiling in his coffin' than upon a Presbyterial ordination administer baptism or the Lord's Supper to a Methodist congregation." (Hist. Method., pp. 181, 182.)

He not only said he would rather see his friend "smiling in his coffin" than to see him a Presbyterian preacher; but he likewise said he would rather see his children Roman Catholics than Dissenters. Skeats says: "Charles, who was always 'harping on the Established Church,' remarked that he would sooner see his children Roman Catholics than Protestant Dissenters. He applied, publicly, in one of his sermons, the shipwreck of Paul to the difficulty of being saved out of the Church of England." (Hist. Free Churches of Eng., p. 382.)

His biographer sums up his life in these words: "He denied the validity of baptism when administered by any except the Episcopal clergy, to whatever section of the church universal the administrator might belong; calling it 'lay baptism,' and urging upon those who had received it the necessity of being re-baptized. Healthy children, he insisted upon baptizing by trine immersion, plunging them three times into the water." (Jackson's Life of Charles Wesley, vol. 1, p. 54.)

Charles Wesley was a "close communionist" with a vengeance. Indeed, I have shown by undoubted authority that the whole Wesley family were close communionists.

The first Methodist Conference believed as Mr. Wesley did on this subject. The ten preachers present did not consider themselves as having received episcopal ordination: and hence had no right to administer baptism or the Lord's Supper. To this end they passed the following rules: "1. Every preacher who acts in connection with Mr. Wesley and the brethren who labor in America is strictly to avoid administering the ordinances of baptism and the Lord's Supper. 2. All people among whom we labor are to be earnestly exhorted to attend the church (meaning, of course, the Episcopal church), and to receive the ordinances there; but in a particular manner to press the people in Maryland and Virginia to the observance of this minute." (McTyeire's Hist. Meth., p. 276.)

Previous to this time the Methodists did not pretend to be anything except a society in the Church of England; but the Revolutionary War had overthrown that Church in America. The Methodists were thus left without a church or ordinances. An appeal was made to Mr. Wesley. He hesitated. At length Mr. Wesley selected a young man, and wrote Dr. Lowth, Bishop of London, and asked for his ordination, which the Bishop did not grant. "Thereupon, on August 10, 1780, he wrote a letter to the bishop, pointing out the great evil he had done to spiritual religion in America by that refusal. Before finishing his letter, Mr. Wesley thus plainly writes his mind: Your lordship did not see good to ordain the pious young man I recommended, but your lordship did see good to ordain and send into America other persons who knew something of Greek and Latin, but who knew no more of saving souls than of catching whales. In this respect I mourn for poor America." (McTyeire's Hist. Method., p. 318.)

On account of this peculiar state of affairs in America there was great strife among the Methodists. Stevens gives this account: "Meanwhile none of our preachers being ordained, the societies were dependent upon the clergy of the English church in this country for the sacraments.

THE METHODISTS. 129

At the Revolution most of these left the country, and the Methodists were then deprived of the sacraments. Many insisted upon having them without ordination. A general strife ensued, a large portion of the Southern church revolted. A compromise was effected till they could apply to Mr. Wesley for a more thorough arrangement, with powers to ordain and minister the sacraments. In meeting their demand he ordained and sent over Dr. Coke, with episcopal powers, under the name of superintendent, to ordain Francis Asbury a 'joint superintendent' and ordain the preachers to the office of deacons and elders." (Church Polity, pp. 86, 87.) But the whole thing resulted in the declaration that baptism administered by a man with episcopal ordination was necessary to the Lord's Supper.

The so-called ordination, mentioned above, of Dr. Coke by Mr. Wesley is one of the strangest events in history; but it reveals a chapter on close communion unparalleled in the history of the world.

To understand these matters it must be recollected that Dr. Coke was a man of great ambition; and the obtaining the office of a bishop seems to have been his absorbing aim. I wish to state that only which can be clearly proved. Tyerman, who is himself a noted Methodist, says: "With the highest respect for Dr. Coke, and his general excellences, it is no detraction to assert, that he was dangerously ambitious, and that the height of his ambition was to be a bishop." (Life of Wesley, vol. 3, p. 434.)

Things had reached such a pass among the Methodists of the United States that something must be done. There was no one authorized among them to administer baptism or the Lord's Supper. Wesley was already well advanced in years, and so Dr. Coke wrote Mr. Wesley proposing to go to America for him. Wesley at length decided to make Coke "superintendent" of the work in America. Such a high-churchman was Dr. Coke that he appears to have had scruples whether Mr. Wesley had any such power. Stevens says: "When Mr. Wesley proposed to Dr. Coke his ordination to this new office, some six or seven months before it was confirmed, the doctor was startled (as Drew tells us in his life of Coke), and doubted Wesley's authority to ordain him, as Wesley himself was not a bishop." (Church Polity, pp. 92, 93.)

These scruples appear to have speedily passed away, and Dr. Coke was not only anxious to be "superintendent," but bishop as well. He then applied to Wesley for ordination, but Wesley possessed no such power. Tyerman says: "There can be no question that there is force in Dr. Whitehead's critique, that 'Dr. Coke had the same right to ordain Mr. Wesley, that Mr. Wesley had to ordain Dr. Coke.'" Our author continues:

THE METHODISTS. 131

"The ordination of Dr. Coke is a perplexing puzzle. Coke had been already ordained a deacon and a priest of the Church of England; and hence, his ministerial status was the same as Wesley's. What further ordination was needed? Wesley intended none; but Coke wished it." (Life of Wesley, vol. 3, p. 432.)

Upon this subject Dr. Whitehead, who wrote the official Life of Wesley, says: "That the person who advised the measure, would be proved to have been a felon to Methodism, and to have struck an assassin's knife into the vitals of its body." (Hawk's Eccl. Hist., vol. 1, p. 171.)

Wesley was bitterly opposed to the office of bishop. In a letter to Francis Asbury, dated London, September 20th, 1788, he says: "How can you, how dare you suffer yourself to be called a bishop? I shudder and start at the very thought. Men may call me a knave or a fool; a rascal, a scoundrel, and I am content: but they shall never, by my consent, call me a bishop. For my sake, for God's sake, for Christ's sake, put a full end to this."

The facts are these: Wesley wanted some one to go to America, and Dr. Coke wanted to go. Dr. Coke stated that if Wesley would send him as his official representative he would be received in America. To this end Wesley privately laid his hands upon Coke and called him "superintendent." Wesley did not ordain him, nor any one else, bishop; nor was Coke called a bishop for a number of years, and never by Wesley's authority.

Tyerman undoubtedly gives a correct history of this affair. He says: "Shall Wesley or some one else go from England to give them ordination? Wesley, a man of action, decided to send Coke, and Coke consented; but before starting, he wished to have an additional ordination himself. What was that ordination to be? The only one possible was this. Wesley was the venerable father of the 15,000 Methodists in America. He was not able to visit them himself; but sends them Dr. Coke. The doctor pretends, that it is more than possible, that some of the American preachers and societies will refuse his authority. To remove this objection, Wesley, at Bristol, in a private room, holds a religious service, puts his hands upon the head of Coke, and (to use his own words) sets him apart as a *superintendent* of the work in America, and gives him a written testimonial to that effect. This was all that Wesley did, and all that Wesley meant; but we greatly doubt that it was all that the departing envoy wished." (Life of Wesley, vol. 3, p. 433.)

Dr. Coke not only knew that Wesley did not ordain him a bishop, but made repeated efforts to be made a bishop of the Episcopal Church. I shall mention some of these attempts.

Dr. Coke appealed to Bishop White of Pennsylvania to give him Episcopal ordination. Here is a part of his letter to the bishop: "He (Mr. Wesley) did indeed solemnly invest me, so far as he had the right so to do, with Episcopal authority, but did not intend, I think, that our entire separation should take place. * * * Our ordained ministers will not, ought not, to give up the right of administering the sacraments: I do not think the generality of them, perhaps none of them, would refuse to submit to a reordination, if other hinderances (a classical education) were removed out of the way." (White's Memoirs of the Protestant Epis. Church, pp. 424-9.) He further requested that Bishop White would burn this letter.

Tyerman, in commenting upon this, says: "Some years after this, Coke, unknown to Wesley and Asbury, addressed a confidential letter to Dr. White, bishop of the Protestant Episcopal Church of Pennsylvania, which, if it meant anything, meant that he would like the Methodists of America to be reunited to the English Church, on condition that he himself was ordained to be their bishop." (Life of Wesley, vol. 3, p. 434.)

On March 29th, 1799, Dr. Coke wrote the Bishop of London, and asked him for episcopal ordination. In that letter he says: "A very considerable part of our society have imbibed a deep prejudice against receiving the Lord's Supper from the hands of immoral clergymen. The word immoral they consider in a very extensive sense, as including all those who frequent card-tables, balls, horse-racing, theaters, and other places of fashionable amusements. I have found it in vain to urge to them that the validity of the ordinance does not depend upon the piety or even the morality of the minister; all of my arguments have had no effect. In consequence of this, petitions were sent, immediately after the death of Mr. Wesley, from different Societies to our Annual Conferences, requesting that they might receive the Lord's Supper from their own preachers, or such as Conference might appoint to administer it to them. For two years this point was combatted with success; but some of our leading friends conceiving that a few exempt cases might be allowed, opposition to the measure was overruled. These exempt cases, as had been foreseen, annually increased; so that now a considerable number of our body have deviated in this instance from the Established Church; and I plainly perceive, that this deviation, unless prevented, will, in time, bring about a universal separation from the Establishment.

"But how can this be prevented? I am inclined to think, that if a given number of our leading preachers, proposed by our General Conference, were to be ordained, and permitted to travel through our connection, and administer the Sacraments to those societies who have been thus prejudiced as above, every difficulty would be removed. I have no doubt that the people would be universally satisfied. The men of greatest influence in the connection would, I am sure, unite with me; and every deviation from the Church of England would be done away.

"In a letter which a few months past I took the liberty of writing to your lordship, on the business of our societies in Jersey, I observed, that for a little time I had been warped from my attachment from the Church of England, in consequence of my visiting the States of America; but like a bow too much bent, I have again returned. But I return with a full conviction that our numerous societies in America would have been a regular Presbyterian church, if Mr. Wesley and myself had not taken the steps which we judged it necessary to adopt." (Drew's Life of Coke, pp. 289, 290.) The Doctor then set the time that he would call upon the bishop and receive ordination. The bishop waited nearly a month before he replied to this letter, then declined to accede to this request, and stated that if they had "such tender consciences" about receiving the Lord's Supper from "immoral men" the same thing ought to apply to ordination as well.

These failures did not discourage him. Almost to the hour of his death, Dr. Coke knocked at the Episcopal door for ordination. Tyerman gives these further examples: "In 1794, he secretly summoned a meeting, at Litchfield, of the most influential of English preachers, and passed a resolution, that the conference should appoint an order of bishops, to ordain deacons and elders, he himself, of course, expecting to be a member of the prelatical brotherhood. And again, it is a well-known fact, that, within twelve months of his lamented death, he wrote to the Earl of Liverpool, stating that he was willing to return most fully into the bosom of the Established Church, on condition, that his royal highness the Prince Regent, and the government would appoint him their bishop in India. These are unpleasant facts; which we would rather have consigned to oblivion, had they not been necessary to vindicate Wesley from the huge inconsistency of ordaining a co-equal presbyter to be a bishop." (Life of Wesley, vol. 3, pp. 434, 435.)

The point I make is very clear. Dr. Coke did not think a man that had not received Episcopal ordination had a right to administer baptism and the Lord's Supper. In fact no man's high-church zeal outran his. Drew says of him: "In describing the character of the clergy of America, he seems to have forgotten that he was still an Englishman; and he introduced his observations in a manner, that would seem, from his omitting, in the ardour of his zeal, the restrictive application, to imply an universal characteristic. On the subject of an Episcopal Establishment, under the immediate auspices of the State, he was equally negligent in marking the peculiar situations of Great Britain and the United States; and he seemed hardly to be aware of the difficulty of vindicating the appendages of monarchy upon republican ground, or of expatiating upon the rights of independence on the continent without interfering with the regulations established in his native land." (Life of Coke, p. 97.)

The very Discipline that he prepared was of the closest order. This is found in it: "Persons not belonging to the society may be admitted, provided they procure a recommendation from an Elder or a Deacon. But in no case is any person to be admitted, who is guilty of practices, for which, if a member he would be excluded from a Methodist society." (Drew's Life of Coke, p. 113.) The plain English of this is: An outsider may commune with us, provided he is willing to be a Methodist.

CHAPTER X.

THE TERMS OF COMMUNION IN THE METHODIST CHURCH. ARE THE METHODISTS CLOSE COMMUNIONISTS? ASBURY AND HEDDING. THE DISCIPLINE. LIVING BISHOPS. WATSON AND OTHERS.

ASBURY, who was the second bishop of the Methodist Church, was likewise a "close communionist." He had serious doubts about being ordained as "superintendent" by Dr. Coke. Dr. Hawks says: "On the 3d of November, 1784, Dr. Coke arrived in New York, and on the 14th met Mr. Asbury for the first time, who, upon learning of the new plan expressed strong doubts concerning it." (Hist. Eccl. U. S., vol. 1, p. 166.)

When some of the Methodists had revolted against the Episcopalians, and went about to ordain preachers of their own, it was Asbury who opposed and finally defeated the measure. Says Drew: "Mr. Asbury in the meanwhile, who had not yet shaken off the rusty fetters of 'Apostolic Succession,' found himself comparatively deserted by those whose respect for him still remained undiminished. Against the illegality of their proceedings he bore a public testimony, denying the authority by which the preachers acted, and declaring the ordination to which they had given existence, invalid. With individuals his arguments had weight, and many hesitated to follow the measure they had adopted. In this manner he proceeded, until he had proselyted some, had silenced others, and had shaken the faith of all; so that at a subsequent conference, he found means to procure a vote, which declared the former ordination unscriptural."

It will thus appear that Asbury, like Coke, was a believer in an Episcopal ordination as necessary for the administration of baptism and the Lord's Supper.

In their notes on the Discipline Asbury and Coke say: "We must also observe, that our elders should be very cautious how they admit to the communion persons who are not in our society. It would be highly injurious to *our* brethren if we suffered any to partake of the Lord's Supper with them whom we would not readily admit into our society on application made to us. Those whom we judge unfit to partake of our profitable, *prudential* means of grace, we would most certainly think improper to be partakers of an ordinance which has been expressly instituted by Christ himself." (History of the Discipline, p. 377.)

Now if this bit of history proves anything, it is, that the Wesleys, Coke and Asbury, were all close communionists in the strictest sense of that term. They regarded Baptists and Presbyterians as unbaptized, excluded Dissenters from the table, and were zealous for all other high-church practices. In fact for seven years after its organization the Methodist Church was without the sacraments, baptism and the Lord's Supper, simply because they would not recognize any save Episcopal ordination. This they did not have and could not get. If the Methodists do not hold these things to-day, they have only the Episcopalians to thank for not bestowing upon them the much coveted gift of Episcopal ordination.

But close communion did not stop here. The old Discipline was very stringent in its requirements. The following relates to the Lord's Supper:

"Question. Are there any directions to be given concerning the administration of the Lord's Supper?

"Answer 1. Let those who have scruples concerning the receiving of it kneeling, be permitted to receive it either standing or sitting.

"2. Let no person that is not a member of *our* church be admitted to the communion, without examination, and some token given by an elder or deacon.

"3. No person shall be admitted to the Lord's Supper among us, who is guilty of any practice for which we would exclude a member of our church."

Certainly no Baptist or Presbyterian would care to be examined by an "elder or deacon." Bishop Hedding in an able discourse says of these rules: "Is it proper for a preacher to give out a general invitation in the congregation to members in good standing in other churches to come to the Lord's Supper?" To this the Bishop gives the following answer: "No; for the most unworthy persons are apt to think themselves in good standing, and sometimes persons who are not members of any church will take the liberty from such an invitation to come. And again, there are some communities called churches, which, from heretical doctrines or immoral practices, have no claim to the privileges of Christians, and ought not to be admitted to the communion of any Christian people. The RULE in that case is as follows: 2. Let no person be admitted to the communion without examination, and some token given by an elder or deacon. 3. No person shall be admitted to the Lord's Supper among us who is guilty of any practice for which we would exclude a member of our church." (Administration of the Discipline, pp. 72, 73.)

But the most stringent of these rules is still in force. The Discipline *now* says: "No person shall be admitted to the Lord's Supper among us who is guilty of any practice for which we would exclude a member of our church." (Discipline, 1890, sec. 408, p. 257.)

The question arises: For what would a member be excluded from the Methodist Church? The Discipline answers: A member shall be excluded for endeavoring "to sow dissension in any of our Societies by inveighing against either our doctrine or discipline." (Dis., 1890, sec. 283, p. 165.)

It is said of a traveling preacher: "What shall be done with those ministers or preachers who hold and disseminate, publicly or privately, doctrines which are contrary to our Articles of Religion?

"Let the same process be observed as in the case of immorality." (Sec. 260, p. 152.)

Now read this: "No person shall be admitted to the Lord's Supper among us who is guilty of any practice for which we would exclude a member of our Church." (Dis., sec. 408, p. 257.)

It is quite certain that if these rules were enforced that no one save a Methodist could approach a Methodist communion table. There are many things a Baptist would reject in the Discipline and Articles of Faith. The Presbyterians could not abide the Arminianism and Episcopacy of the book. The truth is that a man holding the Presbyterian view of the Scriptures would be excluded from a Methodist

Church, on the enforcement of these rules, as *immoral*. And the Discipline expressly says that if a man holds views contrary to the Articles of Faith he shall not approach the Lord's Table.

I suppose that no creed in Christendom has been so often revised and radically changed as has been the Methodist Discipline. With all of its changes and emendations it is still a close communion book. I shall mention other particulars.

1. The Methodists are exclusive in dress. "The putting on of gold and costly apparel" is forbidden. (Sec. 29, p. 30.) The older Disciplines went so far as to prescribe the cut of a woman's bonnet and the number of ruffles on her dress.

2. The Methodists are exclusive in their class-meetings. "Question 1. What directions are given concerning class-meetings? Answer 1. Let *the membership of every church*, wherever it is practicable, be divided into smaller companies, called classes, according to their respective places of abode; and let the *members* be exhorted to attend the meeting of the same." (Sec. 229, p. 135.)

3. The Methodists are exclusive in their love feasts. "Question: What directions are given concerning love feasts? Answer 1. Love feasts shall be held quarterly, or at such other times as the preacher in charge may consider expedient, *with closed doors*, to which, besides Church-mem-

bers, other serious persons may be admitted by him." (Sec. 227, p. 134.)

4. The Methodist church is exclusive in song books. Let the people "use our own Hymn and Tune Books." (Sec. 223, p. 133.)

5. The Methodist church is exclusive in trading. "It is expected of all who continue in these societies that they should continue to evidence their desire of salvation.

"By doing good, especially to them that are of the household of faith, OR GROANING TO BE SO; employing them preferably to others, buying one of another, helping each other in business; and so much the more because the world will love its own, and them *only*." (Sec. 29, pp. 30, 31.)

This is a remarkable case of boycotting.

6. The Methodists are exclusive in their Sunday-schools. "Question: What directions shall be given concerning Sunday-schools?

"Answer 1. Let Sunday-schools be formed in *all our* congregations where ten persons can be collected for that purpose; and let mission schools be formed wherever practicable.

"Answer 2. Let all the Sunday-schools connected with our congregations be *under the control of our own church;* and *let them use our own Catechisms, Question Books, and periodical literature.*

"Answer 3. The *Quarterly Conference* of each circuit and station *shall be a Board of Managers,* having the supervision of all of the Sunday-schools within its bounds. It shall elect at the fourth Quarterly Conference of each year, on nomination of the preacher in charge, a superintendent for each Sunday-school under its care: provided, that when a vacancy occurs in the superintendency of any Sunday-school during the interim of the Quarterly Conference, the preacher in charge shall appoint a superintendent to serve until the meeting of the next Quarterly Conference: and provided, also, that the preacher in charge shall appoint a superintendent for any new school that may be organized between the meetings of the Quarterly Conference.

"Answer 4. It shall be the duty of the preacher in charge of every circuit and station to be present in all of the Sunday-schools in his charge as often as practicable, to catechise the children, to preach to them as often as convenient, to exhort them to attend regularly upon divine service, to *see that they are instructed in the doctrines and usages of our Church*, and to look after their spiritual welfare as a part of his regular pastoral charge. He shall also lay before the Quarterly Conference, at each quarterly meeting, to be entered upon its journal, a written statement of the number and state of the Sunday-school in his charge, and the pastoral instruction of children, and make a report of the same to his Annual Conference."

Everything about this Sunday-school has the principle of close communion.

Here are six specifications of close communion. They cover the most minute details of human life, even down to the minor particular of wearing apparel. As long as these rules and regulations stand on the Methodist law book it does not become them to discuss Baptist close communion.

It is so understood by the Bishops.

Rev. Thos. Bowman, D.D., Bishop of the M. E. Church, says:

St. Louis, May, 31, 1892.

Dear Brother: The following are the words we use, when inviting people to the sacrament of the Lord's Supper: "Ye that do truly and earnestly repent of your sins and are in love and in charity with your neighbors and intend to lead a new life, following the commandments of God and walking from henceforth in his holy ways; draw near with faith, and take this Holy Sacrament to your comfort."

From this you will see:

1. That we expect those who come to be Christians.

2. We suppose them to be baptized.

3. As a rule we expect them to be members of some church. In our church, those who are probationers are included.

With best wishes yours,

Thos. Bowman.

Rev. E. R. Hendrix, Bishop of the M. E. Church South, says:

KANSAS CITY, MO., May 12th, 1892.

MR. J. T. CHRISTIAN, Jackson, Miss.:

Dear Sir: In answer to yours of the 5th inst., which came during my absence from home, I will say that our invitation to the Lord's Supper is in this language: "Ye that do truly and earnestly repent of your sins, and are in love and charity with your neighbors, and intend to lead a new life, following the commandments of God and walking from henceforth in his holy ways, draw near with faith, and take the holy sacrament to your comfort, and make your humble confession to Almighty God, meekly kneeling upon your knees."

As you will see such an invitation implies a holy life which is supreme. While as a rule only church members (which means baptized persons) partake of the Lord's Supper, yet where a penitent is deeply perplexed and is slow to obtain pardon for his sins, a wise pastor sometimes brings him to the test of the sacrament where in the very act of presenting himself there have been cases of happy conversion, the weak faith being strengthened by the outward and visible signs which enable the penitent to discern the Lord's body.

Yours sincerely,

E. R. HENDRIX.

Or as Bishop J. C. Keener, of New Orleans, writes under date of May 12th, 1892: "No change in the conditions for the last one hundred years."

I will quote two recent writers of the Methodist Church.

Rev. Miles G. Bullock, a prominent Methodist writer of New York, says on this subject in a book with the title, "What Christians Believe": "A Baptist maintains that only believers are to be baptized; hence, infant baptism is nonsense; baptism is baptism by immersion; baptized believers only have any right to the Lord's Supper. How can they, therefore, consistently invite or allow me, having only been sprinkled, and that in infancy, to commune with them? Do they keep me away from the Lord's Table, or is it I who am responsible for neglect of this sacrament, having refused to comply with the essential conditions of its reception? Close communion, as it is generally termed, is the only logical and consistent course for Baptist churches to pursue. If their premises are right, the conclusion is surely just as it should be. 'But,' says one, whose prejudices are all awake, 'why will they not commune with those believers in other churches who have been immersed?' For the consistent reason that such persons have violated the New Testament order in communing with unbaptized believers, and are, therefore, not considered in good standing. They do not feel

THE METHODISTS. 149

willing to countenance such laxity in Christian discipline. Let us honor them for stern steadfastness in maintaining what they believe to be a Bible precept, rather than criticise and censure because they differ with us concerning the intent and mode of Christian baptism, and believe it to be an irreparable condition of coming to the Lord's Supper."

The New York *Christian Advocate* said in an editorial in 1884: "We do not believe in administering the sacrament to children, nor to any one that, on their personal character, moral or mental, are not, in the opinion of the church, suitable to be received intelligently on probation in the church, with reference to admission into full membership, if they live consistent Christian lives and show that they have been converted."

It is therefore evident not only that the Methodist Church has rules governing the approach to the Lord's table, but if they were enforced, no one save a Methodist could commune at it.

If any thing is proved by these extracts it is that every church has the right to judge of the qualifications of those who come to its table. I would go further and state that the Lord's Supper is placed within, and directly under the control of the church. "The eucharist," says Dr. Hibbard, "is a church ordinance and as such can be properly participated in only by church members. As a church ordinance, it never can be carried out of the church. This is so evident that no words can make it more plain, or add to its force." (Baptism, p. 185).

In principle are the Baptists any more close than are the Methodists? I shall let Dr. Hibbard give answer. He says: "Before entering upon the argument before us, it is just to remark *that in one principle the Baptists and Pedobaptists churches agree. They both agree in rejecting from communion at the table of the Lord and in denying the rights of church fellowship to all who have not been baptized.* Valid baptism they consider as essential to constitute visible church membership. This also we hold. The only question, then, that here divides us, is, What is essential to valid baptism? The Baptists, in passing the sweeping sentence of disfranchisement upon all other Christian churches, have acted upon a principle held in common with all other Christian churches; viz., that baptism is essential to church membership. They have denied our baptism, and, as unbaptized persons, we have been excluded from their table. That they err greatly in their views of baptism, we, of course believe.

"*But according to their views of baptism, they certainly are consistent in restricting thus their communion.* We would not be understood as passing a judgment of approval upon their course; but we say, their views of baptism force them upon the ground of strict communion, and herein *they act upon the same principle as other churches*, i.e., they admit only those whom they deem baptized persons to the communion table. Of course they must be their own judges as to what baptism is. It is evident that, according to our views of baptism, it is equally evident, they can never reciprocate the courtesy. AND THE CHARGE OF CLOSE COMMUNION IS NO MORE APPLICABLE TO THE BAPTISTS THAN TO US INASMUCH AS THE QUESTION OF CHURCH FELLOWSHIP WITH THEM IS DETERMINED BY AS LIBERAL PRINCIPLES AS IT IS WITH ANY OTHER PROTESTANT CHURCH, so far, I mean, as the present subject is concerned; i.e., it is determined by valid baptism." (Hibbard on Bapt., P. 2, p. 174.)

Richard Watson, and Methodism boasts of no greater, lays down these rules to govern the Lord's Supper:

"1. The very nature of the ordinance of the Lord's Supper excludes from participating in it not only open unbelievers, but all who reject the doctrine of the atonement made by the vicarious death of Christ for 'the remission of sins.' Such persons have indeed tacitly acknowledged this, by reducing the rite to a mere commemoration of the fact of Christ's death, and of those virtues of humility, benevolence, and patience, which his sufferings called forth. If, therefore, the Lord's Supper be in truth much more than this;

if it recognize the sacrificial character of Christ's death, and the doctrine of faith in his blood, as necessary to our salvation, this is 'an altar of which they have no right to eat' who reject these doctrines; and from the Lord's table all such persons ought to be repelled by ministers, whenever, from compliance with custom, or other motives, they would approach it.

"2. It is equally evident that when there is no evidence in persons of true repentance for sin, and of desire of salvation, according to the terms of the Gospel, they are disqualified from partaking at 'the table of the Lord.' They drink and eat unworthily, and fall therefore into 'condemnation.' The whole act is indeed on their part an act of bold profanation or of hypocrisy; they profess by this act to repent, and have no sorrow for sin; they profess to seek deliverance from its guilt and power, and yet remain willingly under its bondage; they profess to trust in Christ's death for pardon, and are utterly unconcerned concerning either; they profess to feed upon Christ, and hunger and thirst after nothing but the world; they place before themselves the sufferings of Christ; but when they 'look upon him whom they have pierced,' they do not 'mourn because of him,' and they grossly offend the all-present majesty of heaven, by thus making light of Christ, and grieving the Holy Spirit.

"3. It is a part of Christian discipline in every

THE METHODISTS. 153

religious society to prevent such persons from communicating with the Church. They are expressly excluded by apostolic authority, as well as by the original institution of this sacrament, which was confined to Christ's disciples; and ministers would partake of other men's sins, if knowingly they were to admit to the Supper of the Lord those who in their spirit and lives deny him." (Inst. Theol., vol. 2, pp. 669, 670.)

The New York *Christian Advocate*, the ablest Methodist paper on this continent, says: "There is no authority, Scriptural or Methodistic, for making the invitation general. The man who will not subject himself to the discipline of the Christian Church, and ally himself with its members, has no right to ask or receive communion at its hands. The course pursued by some ministers degrades the church and sacraments. Every person should be formally recognized as a disciple of Christ; it should not be left to his own judgment. Years ago a minister said: 'We sit in judgment upon no one. If in his heart he feels that he loves the Lord, he can come and commune with us.' And the meanest loafer in town, in debt to half of the church for money spent upon his vices, unkind to his heart-broken wife, and expelled from another church, marched forward with a smirk upon his face to take communion. After what the minister had said, he could not consistently refuse him, but nearly every important member of the church expressed his disapproval in such terms that the experiment was not tried there again."

It would, therefore, be wise for some persons to learn this further lesson given by the New York *Christian Advocate:* "The regular Baptist churches in the United States may be considered to-day as practically a unit on three points—the non-use of infant baptism, the immersion of believers only upon a profession of faith, and the administration of the holy communion to such only as have been immersed by ministers holding these views. In our opinion the Baptist Church owes its amazing prosperity largely to its adherence to these views. In doctrine and government, and in other respects, it is the same as the Congregationalists. In numbers, the regular Baptists are more than six times as great as the Congregationalists. It is not bigotry to adhere to one's convictions, provided the spirit of Christian love prevails."

With the above facts before me, taken as they are from the Discipline and the ablest writers of that denomination, I am led to believe, that in principle and often times in practice, the Methodist Church is very stringent in its terms of communion. I am equally sure that the Methodists, if they should carry out their own principles, would be far more stringent than the Baptists. It is also quite certain that the Methodist circuit riders, and some others, who throw down all barriers, and give an indiscriminate invitation for all persons, good and bad, to partake of the Lord's Supper, act contrary to the Discipline and teachings of their church. It is then a point made out that the requirements of the Baptists in their terms of communion, are no more rigid than are the Methodists.

CHAPTER XI.

THE TERMS OF COMMUNION AMONG THE DISCIPLES OR OF THE CHRISTIAN CHURCH. ARE THE DISCIPLES CLOSE COMMUNIONISTS?

THIS denomination believes with all others that faith, baptism, and church membership are prerequisites to the communion. They go further than some and state that baptism is immersion and deny infant baptism. Holding such views, how they can be other than "close communionists," and be at all consistent, I do not know. I do not wish to speculate so I shall let their foremost men answer.

I begin with Alexander Campbell. He says: "We do not recollect that we have ever argued out the merits of this free and open communion system. But one remark we must offer in passing, that we must regard it as one of the weakest and most vulnerable causes ever plead; and that the 'great' Mr. Hall, as he is called, has in his defence of the practice, made it appear worse than before. In attempting to make it reasonable, he has only proved how unreasonable and unscriptural it is." (Mil. Har., vol. 2, p. 393.)

In reply to a question from Mr. Jones of England, Mr. Campbell says: "Your third question is, Do any of your churches admit unbaptized persons to communion, a practice that is becoming very prevalent in this country? NOT ONE SO FAR AS IS KNOWN TO ME. I am at a loss to understand on what principle—by what law, precedent or license, any congregation founded upon the apostles and prophets, Jesus Christ being the chief corner stone, could dispense with the practice of the primitive church—with the commandment of the Lord and the authority of his apostles." (Mil. Har., vol. 6, p. 18.)

In his debate with Mr. Rice, Mr. Campbell says: "We have no OPEN COMMUNION with us, as they in England have. The principle is not at all recognized among us. In England there are large communities of free communion Baptists, who admit Pedobaptists as freely as they do the baptized. We have no such a custom among us." (Debate with Rice, p. 810.)

In the *Christian Baptist*, Mr. Campbell says: "But I object to making it a rule, IN ANY CASE, to receive unimmersed persons to church ordinances: 1st. Because it is nowhere commanded. 2nd. Because it is nowhere precedented in the New Testament. 3rd. Because it necessarily corrupts the simplicity and uniformity of the whole genius of the New Testament. 4th. Because it not only deranges the order of the kingdom, but makes VOID one of the most important institutions ever given to man. It necessarily makes IMMERSION of non-effect. 5th. Because in making a canon to dispense with a divine institution of momentous import, they who do so assume the very same DISPENSING POWER which issued in that tremendous apostasy which we and all Christians are laboring to destroy. If a Christian community puts into its magna charta, covenant or constitution, an assumption to dispense with an institution of the Great King, who can tell where this power of granting license to itself may terminate." (Christ. Bapt., vol. 6, Ans. to Query 9, p. 528.)

Mr. Campbell was certainly no open communionist.

The *Apostolic Times*, a very widely circulated paper, says: "I do not believe that the unimmersed can sit at the Lord's table; at least I do not believe that they do it. Hence, with me, a table set by them is not the Lord's table; and I would not eat at it. * * * From the preceding it would appear that I am a close communionist. This I certainly am, in the severest, true sense of the term." (Editorial, February 29th, 1872.)

Another number of the *Apostolic Times* says: "Open communion will not only kill Baptist churches; but any other churches holding immersion as the one baptism, in which it is adopted."

In the *Christian Quarterly*, for January, 1875, Robert Graham, President of Hocker Female

College says: "In regard to what is called open or close communion the position of the Disciples is peculiar. Pedobaptist churches are usually open or free communionists. This they can be in harmony with their principles. All churches agree that baptism is a prerequisite to communion at the table of the Lord; and as Pedobaptists accept sprinkling, and pouring and immersion as valid forms of baptism, they can receive at the table of the Lord any one who has been baptized, and is living a godly life. Baptists, however, do not allow anything to be baptism but the immersion of a believer; and in this the Disciples are in perfect agreement with them; hence neither of the churches can consistently advocate open communion."

The late Isaac Errett, for many years editor of the *Standard*, says: "Restore baptism to its place as the ordinance in which the believing penitent puts on Christ, and receives the assurance of the forgiveness of sins. Restore the Lord's Supper to its place as the weekly feast of *Christians*." By Christians he means only the baptized. (Walks About Jerusalem, p. 147.)

Moses E. Lard says: "In the outset of the reformation, our motto was: And thus saith the Lord for every article of our faith, a precept, or precedent for all we do. In the light of this cherished postulate, what defence can we plead for our act, when we sit down to commune with the unimmersed. * * * But suppose a man to be a true believer in Christ, to be truly penitent, to be sprinkled and not immersed, and sincerely to think this baptism, to be strictly a moral man, and to feel in his heart that he is a Christian—what then? May he not commune? I answer, yes: provided it can be shown that sincerely thinking so transmutes an act of sprinkling into an act of immersion or causes God to accept the thing He has not appointed for the thing he has." (In Quarterly, 1863, pp. 41, 52.)

It seems that some Baptist minister in the East had presided at the communion table in a "Christian Church," and some of the "Disciples" were loudly praising him for liberality. Rev. E. W. Herndon, Editor of the *Quarterly Review*, replies: "A Baptist is a 'brother among brethren' when he will violate his party obligations and partake of the Lord's Supper with the disciples of Jesus. This man knows that his religious organization holds that it is wrong for him to do this thing, yet he does it, and continues to hold his fellowship with it, and receives pay from its members for preaching its doctrines. Is he honest? We have heard that Spurgeon permits members of other religious organizations to commune with him, but not long since he denounced those he called Campbellites as heretics. * * * Our duty is to proclaim the terms of naturalization, and it is God's prerogative to decide who have complied with the terms. We have no right to proclaim the terms, and then say that citizenship may be acquired by other means. According to the above, a Baptist is a 'brother among brethren,' and just as much a citizen of the Kingdom of God as those for whom he was presiding. If he is a 'brother among brethren,' then he is one of the family and our debates with Baptists must cease. If the Baptists will permit it, disciples of Jesus, when living in a locality where there is no congregation of disciples, may and should take membership in a Baptist organization, assist in supporting the pastor and their missionary enterprises, if this position is correct. We do not so read the Bible. It may be possible that these editors are more liberal in their fellowship and fraternity than God. We may be narrow, but we endeavor to be consistent, and we think that we are not narrower than the Word of God." (Christian Review, 1887, p. 637.)

Prof. J. W. McGarvey, of the Bible College, Lexington, Ky., says: "We believe that faith, repentance and baptism are the Scriptural prerequisites to the Lord's Supper, and that no believer is entitled to the ordinance until he has been baptized. We believe the privilege belongs to all baptized believers, and to those who are leading an orderly life, and to none others." (Apostolic Times, November 17th, 1874.)

The *American Christian Review*, Cincinnati, Ohio, says: "It is contrary to the Word of God to break bread and to partake of the cup with persons who have never been immersed into the death of Christ. See Rom. 6."

These writers undoubtedly teach close communion.

CHAPTER XII.

WHAT IS BAPTISM?

FROM the standard authorities of all of these denominations, as well as from the Scriptures, I have demonstrated that conversion, baptism and church membership precede communion. Dr. Knapp sums up the matter when he says: "None but actual members of the Christian church can take part in the Lord's Supper; those who are not Christians are excluded from it. On this point there has been a universal agreement. For by this rite we profess our interest in the Christian church, and our belief in Christ." (Theology, p. 502.)

From this argument there is but one point of divergence, What is church order? If that point were settled, there would be no further controversy. The point of difference is baptism in its act, subjects and design. We regard sprinkling and pouring, infant baptism, and when the rite is administered with the wrong design, as no baptism. Hence we accept the principle of Tertullian: "They who are not rightly baptized, are doubtless not baptized at all." (De Baptismo, cap. xv, p. 230.) So certain are we that those who practice such things have departed from church order that we believe that they have debarred themselves from the table of the Lord. I shall go into no extended arguments on these subjects, but shall content myself with some passing reflections.

The argument for immersion as the act of Christian baptism is overwhelming. Even our English Bible teaches immersion; although it is an Episcopal translation rendered under rules, that forbade the translation of baptize, and commanded that the word should be merely transferred. I have those rules before me. Rules three and four are the ones in point, so I simply quote them: "(3.) The old ecclesiastical words to be kept, namely, as the word 'church' not to be translated congregation, etc. (4.) When any word hath divers significations, that to be kept that has been most commonly used by the most eminent Fathers, being agreeable to the propriety of the place, and the analogy of faith." (See Fuller's Church History of Britain, vol. 3, p. 229.)

That "baptize" was included among these ecclesiastical words is evident from the preface that King James' translators put to their Bible. I find the following: "Avoided the scrupulosity of the Puritans, who leave the old Ecclesiastical words and betake them to others; as when they put washing for baptism, and congregation for church; as on the other side they had shunned the obscurity of the Papists in their azymes, tunike, rational, holocaust, and a number of such like, whereof their late translation is full."

Yet taking King James' translation immersion is the evident meaning of baptism. Read such passages as these: "And there went out unto John all the land of Judea, and they of Jerusalem, and were all baptized of him in the river of Jordan, confessing their sins," Mark 1:5; "And it came to pass in those days, that Jesus came from Nazareth of Galilee, and was baptized of John in Jordan. And straightway coming up out of the water, he saw the heavens opened, and the Spirit like a dove descending upon him," Mark 1:9,10; "And John was also baptizing in Enon near to Salim, because there was much water there: and they came, and were baptized," John 3:23; "And they went down both into the water, both Philip and the eunuch; and he baptized him. And when they were come up out of the water, the Spirit of the Lord caught away Philip," Acts 8:38,39; "Therefore we are buried with him by baptism into death: that like as Christ was raised up from the dead by the glory of the Father, even we also should walk in the newness of life," Rom. 6:4; "One Lord, one faith, one baptism," Eph. 4:5.

I have already showed that baptize was transferred and not translated. It is a Greek word in English dress. Dr. Edward Beecher says of it:

"I remark, then, that to transfer words from one language to another, is not to mistranslate, but simply to take a word from the stores of one language, and by it to enrich those of another. The sense of such a word is to be fixed, as in the sense of all other words, by the association of ideas. For example, to dip, is of Saxon origin, and belongs to the native stores of our language. On the other hand the word *immergo* did not belong to our language, but to the Latin. At length, from a form of this verb, the word immerse was transferred to our language, and *immersio* was transferred to immersion. In like manner baptize and baptism have been transferred from the Greek." (Baptism with Reference to its Modes and Subjects, p. 122.)

We are therefore justified in appealing to the Greek for the original meaning of the word baptize. It will there be found to have a special and not a general meaning. As John Pye Smith says: "The New Testament has no generic term to designate Baptism and the Lord's Supper." (First Lines of Christian Theology, Art. Bapt.) In the original Greek, beyond question, baptize means to dip. I shall quote the two most learned Greek Lexicons published, Liddell and Scott, and Thayer. Liddell and Scott define the word: "To dip in, or under water." Thayer says: "To dip repeatedly, to immerse, to submerge. In the New Testament it is used particularly of the rite of sacred ablution, first instituted by John the Baptist, afterward by Christ's command received by Christians and adjusted to the nature and contents of their religion, viz: an immersion in water."

How immersion was changed into sprinkling is equally evident. The brilliant Pressensè says: "To comprehend the value of this august symbol (baptism), we must consider it under its primitive form. I declare at the outset, that I admit the right of the church to modify the form and rite according to times and places. The new covenant is not bound, as was the old, to a Levitical code which rules absolutely all the details of worship, all religious usages. The details are left to Christian liberty; and forms may be varied, provided the spirit of the gospel is not changed. Let it, then, be well understood that we raise no objection to the actual form of baptism in our churches. We believe that it would be an act of Judaism to protest against it, giving thereby an exaggerated importance to a question of this nature. The West can reproduce with difficulty the ceremonies of the East, and we understand very well that sprinkling has been *substituted* for immersion. Nevertheless, to seize with entire clearness the primary idea of the sacrament of regeneration, we must in some way make a primitive baptism assist us. The neophyte was first plunged into the water; and then, when he had emerged, he received the imposition of hands. These two acts of baptism represented the two grand sides of the Christian life—repentance and faith, death and the new life. The neophyte is buried under the waters in sign of his voluntary death to self, in which every serious conversion begins: he becomes one who is planted in the crucifixion of his Saviour. Then he emerges to light in sign of his inward renewal: he becomes one who is planted in the resurrection of Jesus Christ. Thus is figured in a manner the most expressive and solemn all this grand drama of regeneration." (For further information on this subject consult the author's work: Immersion, the Act of Christian Baptism, Baptist Book Concern, Louisville, Ky.)

The Scriptures are equally opposed to infant baptism. The commission under which we baptize reads: "Go ye therefore and teach all nations, baptizing them into the name of the Father, and of the Son, and of the Holy Ghost: teaching them to observe all things whatsoever I have commanded you: and, lo, I am with you alway, even unto the end of the world. Amen." (Matt. 28:19,20.) Mark's words are: "Go ye into all the world, and preach the gospel unto every creature. He that believeth and is baptized shall be saved; but he that believeth not shall be damned." (Mark 16:15,16.) Without doubt, in these passages, discipleship and faith precedes baptism. Infant baptism must, therefore, directly nullify the words of the Lord Jesus.

John the Baptist declared his baptism was "unto repentance," Matt. 3:11; Jesus "made" disciples before he baptized them, John 4:1; and in the apostolic times "they that gladly received the word were baptized," Acts 2:41. From these, and other passages too numerous to quote, it is evident that infant baptism has no place in the Scriptures.

Infant baptism originated not in the Scriptures, but in the unholy doctrine of baptismal salvation. In Lecky's "History of Rationalism" occur the following burning lines: "According to the unanimous belief of the early church all who were external to Christianity were doomed to eternal damnation, and therefore the newborn infant was subject to the condemnation unless baptism had united it to the church. At a period which is so early that it is impossible to define it (we are able now to define it) infant baptism was introduced into the church; it was universally said to be for the remission of sins, and the whole body of the fathers without exception or hesitation pronounced that all infants who died unbaptized were excluded from heaven. All through the Middle Ages we trace the influence of this doctrine in the innumerable superstitious rites which were devised as substitutes for regular baptism. Nothing, indeed, can be more curious, nothing can be more deeply pathetic than the record of the many ways by which the terror-stricken mothers attempted to evade the awful sentence of the church. Sometimes the baptismal water was sprinkled upon the womb; sometimes the still-born child was baptized in hopes that the Almighty would antedate the ceremony. These and many similar practices continued all through the Middle Ages in spite of every effort to extirpate them, and severest censures were unable to persuade the people that they were entirely ineffectual, for the doctrine of the church had wrung the mother's heart with an agony that was too poignant even for that submissive age to bear. Weak and superstitious women, who never dreamed of rebelling against the teaching of their clergy, could not acquiesce in the perdition of their offspring, and they vainly attempted to escape from the dilemma by multiplying superstitious practices or by attributing to them a more than orthodox efficacy."

It is said that this is not believed among Methodists, Presbyterians and others, "at the present day. I answer that infant baptism is not practiced among Presbyterians, Congregationalists and Methodists to-day as at an earlier time. But much of this superstition still exists; else why are ministers hastily sent for to baptize children supposed to be dying? As churches begin to abandon the doctrine that baptism is necessary to the infant's salvation they begin also to abandon infant baptism. Just in proportion as the New Testament ideas prevail, this rite, which is a survival of heathen superstition and Roman tradition, and is utterly without the warrant either of Scripture or reason, falls into disuse. The recent debates over the Westminster Confession have brought before the minds of all the fact that early Calvinistic theologians taught that dying infants might be sent to perdition, though as non-elect rather than as unbaptized."

Pedobaptists fully acknowledge that the Scriptures are as silent as the grave on the subject of infant baptism. Hear only a few scholars.

Dr. A. T. Bledsoe, and among Southern Methodists there has not arisen a greater, says: "But what we wish, in this connection, to emphasize most particularly, is the wonderful contrast between the silence of Christ and the everlasting clamors of his Church. Though he uttered not one express word on the subject of infant baptism, yet, on this very subject, have his professed followers filled the world with sound and fury. The Apostles imitated his silence. But yet, in spite of all of this, have the self-styled 'successors of the Apostles,' and the advocates of their claims, made the universal Church, and all the ages, ring with controversies, loud and long and deep, respecting the rite of infant baptism. Let us follow, then, step by step, the rise of the traditions of the Church, and the inventions of men, by which the beautifully simple ordinance of Christian baptism has been so frightfully disfigured, and made to obscure the freeness, the fulness, and the glory of the Gospel of Christ, as well as to outrage the reason and moral sentiments of mankind. It will be found, unless we are very greatly mistaken, that the authors of these traditions and inventions, have been wise above what is written, and foolish above what could be conceived." (Southern Review, April, 1874, p. 336.)

Dr. Bennett, a more recent Methodist writer, says: "With the most of theologians the exercise of faith is regarded as the necessary condition of the efficient operation of the sacrament. * * * Thus the first converts, whose names and the circumstances of whose baptism are recorded in the Scriptures, were of adult age. That infants and young children were baptized during the apostolic age is nowhere positively affirmed in the New Testament." (Archæology, pp. 390, 391.)

Dr. Meyer, the most learned of modern commentators, says: "Therefore the baptism of even the children of Christian parents, of which there is not a trace in the New Testament, was not, as Origen supposed, an apostolic custom, inasmuch as it met with early and prolonged resistance;

but it is a practice that arose after the age of the apostles, by a gradual process in connection with the development of church life and of church doctrine. There is no reliable testimony concerning it until the age of Tertullian, who opposed it with earnestness. It was defended, however, by Cyprian; but it was only in the time of Augustine that it became general." (Com. Acts 16:15.)

Dr. Harnack, the foremost living Church Historian, says: "The introduction of the practice of pedobaptism into the church is hidden in obscurity. If it owes its origin to the indispensableness of the same to salvation, this is an argument that the superstitious view of baptism had become greatly strengthened." (Harnack: Lehrbuch der Dogmengeschichte, Bk. 1, ss. 358, 359.)

We think our friends of other denominations are radically wrong on the design of baptism. In some way or another they make baptism essential to salvation. We believe that a man is saved through faith, without works, by the atoning mercy of the Lord Jesus. We do not believe that a man is saved by priestly manipulations, by ordinances, nor by churchly functions. So we stand against baptismal salvation in all of its forms.

That others hold baptismal salvation is beyond doubt.

Episcopalians believe in baptismal salvation.

Nothing is more manifest than that baptismal salvation is taught in the Prayer Book. In the Public Baptism of Infants the minister prays: "Almighty and immortal God, the aid of all who need, the helper of all who flee to thee for succour, the life of those who believe, and the resurrection of the dead; we call upon thee for this infant, that he, coming to the holy baptism, may receive the remission of sin, by spiritual regeneration."

In the Catechism which every one must learn before he is confirmed I find:

"What is your name?

"Answer: N. or M.

"Who gave you this name?

"Answer: My sponsors in baptism; wherein I was made a member of Christ, the child of God, and an inheritor of the kingdom of heaven.

"How many sacraments hath Christ ordained in his church?

"Answer: Two only, as generally necessary to salvation; that is to say, Baptism, and the Supper of the Lord."

And in the Order of Confirmation the Bishop prays: "Almighty and everlasting God, who hast vouchsafed to regenerate these thy servants by water and the Holy Ghost, and hast given unto them the forgiveness of all their sins; Strengthen them, we beseech thee, O Lord, with the Holy Ghost."

There is no kind of doubt that this is baptismal salvation. And this is so understood by Episcopal writers.

Dr. Wall says: "Most of the Pedobaptists go no further than St. Austin does; they hold that God, by his Spirit, does at the time of baptism seal and apply to the infant that is there dedicated to him the promises of the covenant of which he is capable, viz: adoption, pardon of sin, translation from the state of nature to that of grace, etc. On which account the infant is said to be regenerated of (or by) the Spirit." (Hist. Infant Baptism, vol 1, p. 175.)

Lord Macaulay says of the Episcopalian Church: "A controversialist who puts an Arminian sense on her articles and homilies will be pronounced by candid men to be as unreasonable as a controversialist who denies that the doctrine of baptismal regeneration can be discovered in her liturgy." (Hist. Eng., vol. 1, p. 41.)

Presbyterians make baptism a means of grace. They still call baptism and the Lord's Supper by the popish name of "sacraments." The doctrine is thus expressed in the Confession of Faith: "Sacraments are holy signs and seals of the covenant of grace, immediately instituted by God, to represent Christ and his benefits; and to confirm our interests in him, as also to put a visible difference between those that belong unto the church, and the rest of the world; and solemnly to engage them to the service of God in Christ, according to his word." (Article XXVII.)

The view of Calvin is thus stated by Dr. Schaff: "He taught that believers, while they receive with their mouths the visible elements, receive also by faith the spiritual realities signified and sealed thereby—namely, the benefit of the atoning sacrifice on the cross and the life-giving virtue of Christ's glorified humanity in heaven, which the Holy Ghost conveys to the soul in a supernatural manner." Or in the words of Dr. Nevin: "The living energy, the vivific virtue, as Calvin styles it, of Christ's flesh, is made to flow over into the communicant, making him more and more one with Christ himself, and thus more and more an heir of the same immortality that is brought to light in his person."

Or as Dr. Nevin puts it in another place: The Church "makes us Christians by the sacrament of holy baptism, which she always held to be of supernatural force for this very purpose." (Christ. Nurture, p. 97.) If this is not sacramental salvation, I do not know how to name it.

Dr. Guthrie says: "And prone, as we of Scotland are, to boast that our fathers, with Knox at their head, came forth from Rome with less of her old superstitions about them than the most of other churches, to what else than some lingering remains of popery can we ascribe the extreme anxiety which some parents show to have baptism administered to a dying child? Does not this look very like a rag of the old faith? It smells of the sepulcher." (Gos. in Ezek., p. 213.)

Dr. Charles Hodge is good authority. He says: "Baptism, however, is not only a sign and a seal; it is also a means of grace, because in it the blessings which it signifies are conveyed, and the promises of which it is the seal, are assured or fulfilled to those who are baptized, provided they believe." "It does not follow from this that the benefits of redemption may not be conferred on infants at the time of baptism. That is in the hands of God. What is to hinder the imputation to them of the righteousness of Christ, or their receiving the renewing of the Holy Ghost, so that their whole nature may be developed in a state of reconciliation with God? Doubtless this often occurs; but whether it does or not, their baptism stands good; it assures them of salvation if they do not renounce their baptismal covenant." (Syst. Theology, vol. 3, pp. 589, 590.)

Methodists believe in baptismal salvation. They call baptism a sacrament and ascribe to it grace. Sacraments are thus mentioned in the Discipline: "Sacraments, ordained of Christ, are not only badges or tokens of Christian men's profession, but rather they are certain signs of grace, and God's good will toward us, by the which he does work invisibly in us, and doth not only quicken, but also strenghten and confirm our faith in him." (Discipline, p. 18.)

In the Administration of Infant Baptism it is said: "Dearly beloved, forasmuch as all men are conceived and born in sin, and that our Saviour Christ saith, Except a man be born of water and of the Spirit, he cannot enter into the kingdom of God: I beseech you to call upon God the Father, through our Lord Jesus Christ, that of his bounteous goodness he will grant to this child, now to be baptized with water, that which by nature *he* cannot have: that he may be baptized with the Holy Ghost, received into Christ's holy Church, and be made a *lively member* of the same " (Discipline, p. 258.)

How baptism can give to an infant that "which by nature he cannot have" and be "made a lively member of" the Church I do not know. If this is not baptismal salvation I am mistaken. Indeed, Dr. Bledsoe says: "Now the man knows absolutely nothing on the subject of our late article (and had, therefore, better say nothing), who does not know that, the history of infant baptism, is, in a very great measure, the history of baptismal regeneration itself. An edition of Shakespeare's Hamlet, with the part of Hamlet omitted, would not be a more ridiculous production than a history of infant baptism without the introduction of baptismal regeneration." (Southern Review, July, 1874, p. 148.)

Lest I may be mistaken in my view of the Discipline I shall give Wesley's own words. He says: "By baptism, we, who were by 'nature the children of wrath,' are made the children of God. And this regeneration which our church in so many places ascribes to baptism is more than barely being admitted into the Church, though commonly connected therewith; being grafted into the body of Christ's Church we are made the children of God by adoption and grace. This is grounded on the plain words of our Lord, 'Except a man be born again of water and of the Spirit, he cannot enter into the kingdom of God.' (John 3:5.) By water, then, as a means—the water of baptism—we are regenerated or born again; whence it is also called by the Apostles, 'the washing of regeneration.' Our Church therefore ascribes no greater virtue to baptism than Christ himself has done. Nor does she ascribe it to the outward washing, but to the inward grace, which, added thereto, makes it a sacrament. Herein a principle of grace is infused, which will not be wholly taken away, unless we quench the Holy Spirit of God by long continued wickedness." (Doctrinal Tracts, pp. 248, 249.)

The above language cannot be explained so that it will not teach baptismal salvation. Tyerman thus comments upon it: "This is strong and somewhat startling language, and yet not really stronger than Wesley used in the sermon on the New Birth." "In reference to infants he unquestionably held the high-church doctrine of his father. It is no part of our proposed task either to justify or to condemn this opinion; our sole object is honestly to relate the facts." (Life of Wesley, vol. 2, pp. 264, 265.)

If there be no sacramental efficacy in these ordinances, why will a Methodist minister hasten at midnight to baptize a dying infant, or give the communion to a dying man? Such a thing has doubtless been done.

Wesley makes baptismal salvation his primary reason for infant baptism, and it is the only ground upon which that rite can be defended. He says: "If infants are guilty of original sin, then they are proper subjects of baptism; seeing, in the ordinary way, they cannot be saved, unless this be washed away by baptism. It has been already proved, that this original stain cleaves to every child of man; and that hereby they are children of wrath, and liable to eternal damnation. It is true, the Second Adam has found a remedy for the disease which came upon all by the offense of the first. But the benefit of this is to be received through the means which he hath appointed; through baptism in particular, which is the ordinary means which he hath appointed for that purpose; and to which God hath tied us, though he may not have tied himself. Indeed, where it cannot be had, the case is different; but extraordinary cases do not make void a standing rule. This therefore is our first ground. Infants need to be washed from original sin; therefore they are proper subjects of baptism." (Doctrinal Tracts, pp. 251, 252.)

The Disciples, or Christian Church, hold the doctrine of baptismal salvation. They make faith, repentance and baptism as the necessary conditions of salvation. This theory debases repentance and faith to mere carnal ordinances; and exalts baptism to an extraordinary degree. That I am not mistaken appears from the following authors:

Alexander Campbell says: "If blood can whiten or cleanse garments, certainly water can wash away sins. There is, then, a transferring of the efficacy of blood to water; and a transferring of the efficacy of water to blood. This is a plain solution of the whole matter. God has transferred in some way, the whitening efficacy, or cleansing power, of water to blood; and the absolving or pardoning power of blood to water. This is done upon the same principle as that of accounting faith for righteousness. What a gracious institution. God has opened a fountain for sin, for moral pollution. He has given it an extension far and wide as sin has spread—far and wide as water flows. Wherever water, faith, and the name of the Father, Son, and Holy Spirit, are, there will be found the efficacy of the blood of Jesus. Yes; as God first gave the efficacy of water to blood, he has now given the efficacy of blood to water. This, as was said, is figurative, but it is not a figure that misleads, for the meaning is given without a figure; viz: immersion for the remission of sins. And to him that made the washing of clay from the eyes, the washing away of blindness, it is competent to make the immersion of the body in water efficacious to the washing away of sin from the conscience." (Millenial Harbinger, Extra, p. 41, 1830, vol. 1.)

Again: "I am bold, therefore, to affirm, that every one who, in the belief of what the Apostle spoke, was immersed, did, in the very instance in which he was put under the water receive the forgiveness of his sins and the gift of the Holy Spirit. If so, then who will not concur with me in saying that Christian immersion is the gospel in water." (Christian Baptist, p. 417.)

Once more: "If being born of water means immersion, as clearly proved by all witnesses; then, remission of sins cannot, in this life, be constitutionally enjoyed previous to immersion. If there be any proposition regarding any item of the Christian institution, which admits of clearer proof, or fuller illustration than this one, I have yet to learn where it may be found." (Christian System, p. 217.)

Scores of other passages can be given from

the writings of Mr. Campbell quite as strong as these.

Isaac Errett, late editor of the *Christian Standard*, says: "The gospel, while proclaiming justification by faith to the sinner, has linked it with the ordinance of baptism, ere the promise 'shall be saved' can be lawfully approached." (Walks About Jerusalem, p. 79.)

O. A. Burgess says: "Is there found anywhere in the New Testament any other institution whatever of God's appointment that sets forth the pardon and acceptance of the sinner under the figure of a birth? * * * There can no more be such a thing as a birth into the kingdom of Christ without water baptism than a child can be said to be born before it has been really born of the mother. It is monstrous to suppose that a single parent is requisite in the new birth and there can be no such thing as the sinner becoming a new creature in Christ Jesus until he comes forth out of the womb of the waters, and having been made dead to sin, is made alive to God." (Thompson-Burgess Debate, pp. 203, 204.)

Moses E. Lard says: "When we cross the line out of the world into the kingdom we cease to be a Jew, cease to be a Gentile; and when we cease to be these we cease to be the children of the wicked one, and become the children of God. But we never cease to be Jew and Gentile till we enter Christ and we never enter him till baptized into him. Then, therefore, do we cease to be the children of Satan and become the children of God." (What Baptism is For, No. 8, pp. 5, 6.)

Robert T. Mathews, Pastor at Lexington, Ky., says: "It is the representation of salvation in reality—the representation of a real cleansing from sin, the representation of a real death to sin, and of a real resurrection to a new life—this spiritual realness alone giving sense and propriety to baptism in its element and action. There is a real presence and power of God in baptism. 'Having cleansed it by the washing of water with the word,' says Paul again, making baptism a picture of purification, and so representing it because something more than water is there— the very word of God in all of its spirit and life, being there. * * * Baptism and salvation coupled in the world-wide commission, baptism and forgiveness heard together in Apostolic preaching, and penitent believers universally, readily, gladly baptized—what was their baptism but a real confirmation of a real salvation in a real experience of their lives?" (Evangelistic Sermons, pp. 123, 124.)

E. W. Herndon says: "Then, a baptism for any other purpose except the remission of sins, is not Christian baptism; then the elements of Christian baptism are, immersion in water of a believer for the remission of sins." (Christian Review, 1888, p. 447.)

WHAT IS BAPTISM? 185

Growing out of these views of baptism we differ with the whole pedobaptist world on the subject of a converted church membership. We believe that God's Word teaches that a man should be a professed Christian before he unites with the church; others believe that the unconverted should join the church as a means of grace. This can be proved from many sources.

Presbyterians hold to an unconverted membership. This is plainly taught by the Presbyterian standards. I read in the Confession of Faith, Article XXV, that the visible church "consists of all those throughout the world, that profess the true religion, *together with their children.*" Again Article XXVIII: "Not only those who do actually profess faith and obedience unto Christ, *but also the infants* of one or both believing parents are to be baptized." In the Longer Catechism, Question 62: "What is the visible church? The visible church is a society made up of all such as in all ages and places of the world do profess the true religion, and *of their children.*" And in the Form of Government, Chapter 2: "A particular church consists of a number of professing Christians, *with their offspring*, voluntarily associated together, for divine worship, and godly living, agreeably to the Holy Scriptures; and submitting to a certain form of government."

The Confession of Faith is confirmed by the highest Presbyterian authorities.

Dr. Charles Hodge says: "The visible Church does not consist exclusively of the regenerate. * * * Our Lord expressly forbids the attempt being made. He compares his external kingdom, or visible Church, to a field in which tares and wheat grow together. He charges his disciples not to undertake to separate them, because they could not, in all cases, distinguish the one from the other. But both may be allowed to grow together unto the harvest." (Systematic Theology, vol. 3, p. 548.)

Dr. A. A. Hodge says: "Children born within the pale of the visible Church are dedicated to God in baptism, when they come to years of discretion, if they be free from scandal, appear sober, and steady, and to have sufficient knowledge to discern the Lord's body, they ought to be informed in their duty and privilege to come to the Lord's Supper." (Page 644.) Again, Dr. Hodge states: "The Baptist churches, denying altogether the right of infant church membership, receive all applicants for the communion as from the world, and therefore demand *positive* evidences of the new birth of all. All the Pædobaptist churches, maintaining that all children baptized in infancy are already members of the church, distinguish between the admission of the children of the church to the communion and the admission *de novo* to the church of the unbaptized alien from the world." (Outlines of Theology, p. 645.)

The Methodists receive unconverted people into their church.

Samuel P. Jones, a distinguished Evangelist of that Church, says: "Down at Huntsville, Ala., one of the leading citizens took me out to one side and said: 'I want to be a Christian, I want to love God and do right, but I can't believe in the divinity of Christ to save my life.' 'Shut your mouth,' I said, 'don't come to me with talk like that. Do just like Christ told you to do and if you don't make the landing I will swim out to you and drown with you. You come to the meeting to-night and be the first one up there when I call for sinners to come forward.' 'If I join the church, Mr. Jones, I can't believe.' 'Shut your mouth, I am prescribing for you, and if you will take my remedy, I will warrant the cure.' He walked up and joined the church that night. I said: 'Well, you have joined the church; you must take up family prayer, and if I call on you to pray in church you must get down and do your level best. I will get you out if you will keep your mouth shut.' I led him out sure enough. That night he took up family prayer and started right. I went back to Huntsville afterward, and asked: 'How is Bro. Ford getting on?' 'He is the best we have.' 'How is he on the divinity?' 'O, he has quit all of that long ago.' If you will give God your heart he will take care of your head. I don't know whether I am orthodox or not, but you can attend to the orthodoxy when I am gone."

The above extract does not read like a chapter from the Acts of the Apostles.

Dr. T. O. Summers says: "We do not mean to say that no one is eligible to baptism who has not an assurance of the pardon of his sin and the regeneration of his nature, through faith in Christ and by the power of the Holy Ghost. Far from it. Of course, those who enjoy the witness of adoption are proper candidates for the ordinance; but so also are all of those who do not enjoy it, yet are desirous of obtaining it and are seeking its possession. Indeed, baptism is admirably suited to their case. It symbolizes the grace which they seek, and thus assists them in their efforts to acquire it: the ordinance thus proves a means whereby the penitent subject receives the inward and invisible grace which it is designed to represent." (Summers on Baptism, pp. 21, 22.)

Holding as we do these widely diverging views from others, views which in their very nature are revolutionary and destructive of the foundation principles of pedobaptism, it would be impossible for us to approach the Lord's Supper with them. We hold that baptism is an absolute qualification to the Lord's Supper, and that sprinkling and pouring, infant baptism and an unconverted membership invalidate the ordinance.

We cannot, therefore, approach the Table with such persons, because thereby we would be partakers of their errors and disobedience. This is not abuse, but the inevitable conclusion of irresistible logic. We are in no wise responsible for this state of things. We put no barriers in the way of a full and free approach to the Lord's Table. We only insist upon the divine order of the Scriptures, and a perfect obedience to the commands of Christ. Our Pedobaptist brethren are responsible for the divisions about the Lord's Supper; for if they will abandon these unscriptural acts and come back to the simplicity of the Gospel we will at once have, "One Lord, one faith, and one baptism."

CHAPTER XIII.

ARE BAPTISTS LACKING IN CHARITY?

THE trouble in the whole communion question lies not in what the Scriptures say about it, but in the anti-scriptural things interjected into the observance of the Lord's Supper. The things which separate the Baptists from others are not the scriptural terms of faith, baptism, church membership and the Lord's Supper; because on these things for the most part we are all agreed, but others insist in either breaking down these barriers to the table, or adding other conditions upon which the Scriptures are silent. It is not bigotry, nor because the Baptists regard all others as heathen, that they keep a close table.

The real difference between Baptists and others is that we hold that the Lord's Supper is a symbolic act; while others hold that the Supper is a means of grace. We hold that it is a church act; others make it a test of Christian fellowship which we never do. This distinction is important, and should constantly be borne in mind.

The charge has been so persistently made that the Baptists by their practice unchristianize all others that I shall let some of our representative men speak.

Rev. J. M. Pendleton, D. D., and he has a right to speak for Baptist people, says: "Baptists do not deny that there are pious men and women in Pedobaptist churches, so called, but they do deny that these churches are formed according to the New Testament model. They are without baptism, and, to use the words of a very distinguished Pedobaptist, Dr. E. D. Griffin, 'where there is no baptism, there are no visible churches.'" (Baptist Principles, p. 172.)

Dr. John A. Broadus, President of the Southern Baptist Theological Seminary, says: "The blessing thus received is not supposed to be essentially different in kind from other spiritual blessings, nor to be associated with mere divine appointment with this particular means of grace. Hence no spiritual loss is necessarily inflicted by failing to invite to this ceremony persons who have made a credible oral profession of faith, but have not yet submitted to the prerequisite ceremony." (Commentary Matt., p. 530.)

Dr. A. Hovey, President of Newton Theological Seminary, says: "Most of the difficulty, if not indeed all of it, which is felt in many minds in relation to our practice as Baptists on the subject of communion at the Lord's table, has arisen from the habit so common among people of confounding Christian communion with Church communion. But they are separate and distinct acts, and ought not to be thus confounded. Let this distinction be fairly understood and properly observed, and we shall hear much less about the 'exclusiveness,' or 'illiberality,' or 'bigotry,' of the Baptists in their spiritual observance of this significant and impressive ordinance of the Gospel. This ordinance is not a test of Christian fellowship, and cannot be so used without perverting its spiritual design."

Prof. T. F. Curtis, an able writer on Communion, says: "True communion is a spiritual—and not a visible thing. It may, in part, be symbolized, as in united prayer, or the Lord's Supper; but no Christian ever yet, on the most extensive sacramental occasion, partook of the same elements with one thousandth part of those with whom he would acknowledge true Christian communion, for this he has, with all saints in heaven, as well as on earth. Nor will the two ever be co-extensive, until he shall sit down with Abraham, Isaac and Jacob, to eat bread in the kingdom of God, at the marriage supper of the Lamb." (Curtis on Communion, p. 35.)

Dr. W. W. Gardner in his able work on Church Communion distinguishes between Christian and church communion. He says: "Christian communion is based upon Christian fellowship. Christian communion extends to all Christians, as such, irrespective of positive ordinances and visible church relations, and embraces all those scriptural acts and exercises by and in which mutual Christian fellowship is expressed and enjoyed. Such communion is fully enjoyed in heaven.

"Church communion is based upon church fellowship, growing out of mutual church relations. Church communion is necessarily limited to the members of the same particular church, for such only sustain mutual church relations. It embraces all of those church acts and privileges by which church fellowship is expressed and enjoyed, and in which none but members of the same church have a right to participate." (Church Communion, pp. 22, 23.)

Dr. P. H. Mell, late Chancellor of the University of Georgia, says: "There can be no scriptural communion excepting as performed by a local gospel church; there can be no local gospel church excepting as composed of individual members; there can be no individual members excepting as they are received on a vote of a local church; none are eligible to be voted for as church members excepting such as have been baptized on a profession of their faith in Christ; nothing is scriptural baptism but immersion upon a profession of faith in Christ; therefore, there can be no scriptural communion which has not been preceded by that ordinance, scriptural immersion." (Ford's Repos., 1878, p. 251.)

Dr. Armitage says: "If fellowship amongst Christians is purchased by sitting with each other at the same table, their love is bought at a very light cost. Oneness with Christ himself, the brotherhood of regeneration by the Holy Spirit, mutual burden-bearing and mutual watch-care, formed the visible bond of fellowship in the Apostolic Churches. This sort of unity cost them something, it was not a vaporing sentiment, it was worth all that it cost. There is not a case in ecclesiastical history where the Supper has held any single congregation together for a day. Churches of all names who celebrate it constantly, live in open contention year by year. The love of Judas for John was cramped into a close corner when they sat at the same table, and ate the sop from the same dish. If Christians are not one on a much higher plane than that of eating and drinking the Supper with each other, their true unity is a hopeless business. In fact, as if to prove the perfect emptiness of this pretension, in some Protestant communions, the Supper itself has been the subject of hot dispute, the chief bone of contention from century to century. The greatest bitterness has been indulged, and anathemas have been bandied about, *pro* and *con*, with a freedom which has marked no other form of discussion, and by men, who regularly meet at the same table." (History Baptists, pp. 146, 147.)

ARE BAPTISTS LACKING IN CHARITY? 195

These are all representative Baptists. They unanimously declare that Baptists pass no sentence of disfranchisement upon any. They believe that the observance of the Lord's Supper is a church ordinance; and they do not extend it beyond their own discipline. The attitude of Baptists on this subject is not one of war but of strict neutrality. Dr. W. C. Wilkinson aptly puts it: "Restricted communion, as practiced by Baptists, is not positive, it is strictly negative. It does not turn away; it simply does not invite. Not inviting, it naturally does not accept invitations. This is really the whole. Restricted communion does nothing more than just maintain this attitude of *not* doing. What could be less offensive?" (Baptist Principles, p. 199.)

With us it is solely a matter of principle, and not of impatience toward others. Dr. Charles Hodge, and I am glad to agree with this eminent Presbyterian, puts this in a strong way. He says: "As Christ is the only head of the Church it follows that its allegiance is to him, and that whenever those out of the Church undertake to regulate its affairs, or to curtail its liberties, its members are bound to obey him rather than men. They are bound by all legitimate means to resist such usurpations, and to stand fast in the liberty where with Christ has made them free. They are under equal obligation to resist all undue assumption of authority by those within the

Church, whether, it be the brotherhood or by individual officers, or by Church councils or courts. The allegiance of the people terminates on Christ. They are bound to obey others only so far as obedience to them is obedience to Him. In the early ages some endeavored to impose on Christians the yoke of the Jewish law. This, of course, they were bound to resist. In the following centuries, and by degrees, the intolerable rituals, ceremonies, fasts, festivals, and priestly, prelatical, and papal assumptions, which oppress so large a part of the Christian world, have been imposed on the people in derogation to the authority of Christ as the sole head of the Church. Councils, provincial and ecumenical, have not only prescribed creeds, contrary to the Scriptures, but also have made laws to bind the conscience, and ordained observances which Christ never enjoined. As Christ is the head of his earthly kingdom, so is he its only lawgiver. He prescribes the terms of admission into his kingdom. These cannot be rightfully altered by any human authority. Men can neither add to them, nor detract from them." (Systematic Theology, vol. 2, pp. 606, 607.)

To all of which we say amen and amen.

CHAPTER XIV.

POSITIVE AND MORAL LAW.

IT has always occurred to me that the advocates of open communion have confounded two things that are widely different—positive and moral law. A moral law is right in the nature of things, and is based upon the immutable and universal principles of truth and justice. On the other hand positive law depends for its authority upon the will of the divine Lawgiver. A moral duty is commanded because it is right, a positive duty is right because it is commanded. A moral law can be obeyed in any way that comports with its spirit; a positive law must be obeyed to its very letter. Of this kind is the observance of the Lord's Supper. We have no choice save to obey the laws of its observance as given in the New Testament.

The Bible puts great emphasis upon the obedience of positive law, and signal have been the punishments inflicted upon those who have violated positive laws. Adam and Eve were driven from the garden as the result of the disobedience of a positive law. Moses was not permitted to see the promised land, and Saul was rejected as King of Israel, all because of disobedience of positive law. These examples show us, that God does not treat lightly a disobedience of any of his commands. It is not a question of "essentials or non-essentials," but how can I obey the Lord.

The Nashville *Christian Advocate*, in a recent editorial laid down the right principle: "But when the proposition is made to change the nature of the Lord's Supper * * * we are against that, now and forever. The canon of accommodating Scripture to our own ideas and changing the constitutional principles in the interest of these views, is rationalism of the most irrational and ruinous kind. When our pet views lead us to criticise the acts of Christ, or change the principles and institutions that he established, it is time for us to halt and retrace our steps and remodel our views."

Bishop Hoadly, of the Episcopal Church, is much to the point. He says: "The partaking of the Lord's Supper is not a duty of itself, or a duty apparent to us from the nature of things, but a duty made such to Christians by the positive institution of Jesus Christ. All positive duties, or duties made such by institution alone, depend entirely on the will and declaration of the person who institutes or ordains them with respect to the real design and end of them, and consequently to the due manner of performing them. For there being no other foundation for them with regard to us, but the will of the institutor, this will must, of necessity, be our sole direction, both as to our understanding their true intent, and practicing them accordingly; because we can have no other direction in this sort of duties, unless we will have recourse to mere invention, which makes them our own institutions, and not the institutions of those who first appointed them. It is plain, therefore, that the nature, the design, and the due manner of the Lord's Supper, must, of necessity, depend on what Jesus Christ, who instituted it, has said about it." (Works, vol. 3, p. 845.)

Just here comes in the mistake, and misapprehension, that exists in so many minds. The "communion of saints" is confounded with the Lord's Supper. Communion of saints is morally right; it is one of the things that will happen of its own accord. I heartily believe in "the communion of saints." But there is a vast difference between Church communion and Christian communion. They are separate and distinct acts and should never be confounded. With the Baptists Church communion is no test of Christian fellowship. Here is where we are often misunderstood. When we gather around the Lord's table it is not to show our love for one another, or our opinion of others; but to show forth the Lord's death till he come again. It is not a test of Christian fellowship at all. Before one calls us illiberal, it would be well for him to understand our position.

There is not an example in the Scriptures where the Lord's Supper is made a test of Christian charity. It is always declared to have another design. In Matt. 26:28,30, it "is *the blood* of the New Testament, which is shed for many for the remission of sins." His atoning blood is the great theme of the Scriptures. In 1 Cor. 11:24-29, is the additional idea that we do this "in remembrance" of what Christ has done for us. The eloquent Melvill caught the spirit of this when he said: "Inasmuch as the bread and the wine represent the body and blood of the Saviour, the administration of this ordinance is so commemorative of Christ's having been offered as a sacrifice, that we seem to have before us the awful and mysterious transaction, as though again were the cross reared, and the words, 'It is finished,' pronounced in our hearing." (Thoughts, p. 240.) Of course we cannot call to recollection brethren who are present with us. We are not to fasten our minds upon our brethren; but upon the all sufficiency of the grace of God and his wonderful work for us.

The very moment we turn our eyes from these lofty themes, and commence to think about ourselves and others, we degrade this memorial feast. It is not of flesh and blood that we are to think, but of the crucified and exalted Christ. It is not a communion, or feast, with our brethren, but with Christ.

This forever does away with much sentimentality about "communion with mother," and my great "liberality," and "how bigoted somebody else is."

CHAPTER XV.

OPEN COMMUNION DESTROYS GOSPEL DISCIPLINE.

ONE of the most fatal objections to open communion is that it breaks down all barriers to the Lord's table, puts it beyond church discipline, and allows the profane and profligate to participate. The Scriptures undoubtedly place the observance of the Supper under the control of the church, and does not extend it beyond the discipline of the church. The church cannot divest itself of responsibility as to the character of its communicants. This is the exact idea of the Greek *Koinonia*, communion.

Here is the authority of the Greek Lexicons.

Thayer says: "Fellowship, association, community, joint participation, intercourse." And the verb is defined, "to make one's self a sharer or partner."

Liddell and Scott says: "Association, partnership, society."

The commentators are also agreed.

Meyer says: "This is the theocratic bond of participation, whereby the man stands bound to the sacrificial altar, who eats of the sacrifice belonging to it as such. The Israelite who refused to eat of the flesh of the sacrifice as such, would thereby practically declare that he had nothing to do with the altar, but stood aloof from the sphere of theocratic connection with it. The man on the other hand, who ate a portion of the flesh offered upon the altar, gave proof of the religious relation in which he stood to the altar itself." (Com. 1 Cor. 10:18.)

The reasoning is conclusive. By participating at the Lord's table together we declare ourselves to be partners, and members of the same organization, or church, and mutually responsible for the right administration of the supper. Only members of the one body, the church, can join in this participation, since no others can be partners in this matter. Paul's reasoning is to the point. He says: "The cup of blessing which we bless, is it not a communion of the blood of Christ? The bread which we break, is it not a communion of the body of Christ? Seeing that we who are many, are one bread and one body: for we all partake of the one bread. Behold Israel after the flesh: have not they which eat the sacrifices communion with the altar? What say I then? That a thing sacrificed to idols is anything, or that an idol is anything? But I say. that the things which the Gentiles sacrifice, they sacrifice to devils, and not to God; and I would not that ye should have communion with devils. Ye cannot drink the cup of the Lord, and the cup of devils: ye cannot partake of the table of the Lord, and of the tables of devils." (1 Cor. 10:16–21, Revised Version.) We are therefore persuaded that the joint participation in the supper means a joint membership in the church.

Dr. Hibbard says: "Those who meet at the Lord's table signify thereby that they have mutual fellowship in the faith, experience and practice of the gospel. Hence, Paul calls it the 'communion of the body and blood of Christ;' 'for we, being many, are one bread and one body; for we are all partakers of that one bread.'" Or says Dr. A. Clarke: "The original would be better translated thus: 'Because there is one bread, or loaf, we, who are many, are one body.' (1 Cor. 10:16,17.) This feasting together declares a community of interest in the merits of the same Jesus whose sacrificial death is exhibited in the distributed elements, and proves the disciples of Christ to be 'ONE BODY.' How, then, can an ordinance which manifestly declares its recipients, though 'many' individuals, to be 'one body,' be administered to those who are not of that body?" (On Baptism, P. 2, p. 185.)

The Advance, of Chicago, an able Congregational journal, reasons thus, in an editorial, November 10th, 1868: "It is a mistake, contrary to the name, the idea, and the apostolic description of this sacrament, to make it only the sign of a faith in Christ, by the individual. The word *koinonia*, communion, contradicts it, meaning the common participation of many in sign of their being one, as Paul explains it, First Corinthians x:16,17, 'The cup of blessing which we bless, is it not the communion of the blood of Christ? The bread which we break, is it not the communion of the body of Christ? For we being many are one bread and one body; for we are all partakers of that one bread.' A church cannot, then, divest itself of all responsibility for fellow communicants. If any ordinance is in meaning and act purely an individual acknowledgment of Christ, in which the recipient alone is concerned, and others are not responsible, baptism may be so considered. The Supper, on the contrary, is the appointed method of expressing our communion with each other; and this is the very ground of our complaint against the Baptists, that by their close communion they withhold the appointed sign of fellowship from visible, professed Christians, who are organized as such into churches, and whose spiritual character they neither deny nor doubt. It is the Lord's table, and we express a general confidence in the Christian character of those who are invited to partake with us, and are bound, therefore, reasonably to protect it from improper approach by requiring that those who come to it should be members of Christian churches."

The *Independent* in an editorial, August 18th,

1892, says: "A leading Baptist paper in the United States says: 'There is for the open communion Baptist nothing to justify a separation from his pedo-Baptist brethren.'

"This is perfectly correct. There is no reason whatever why open communion Baptists, like the free Baptists, for example, should form a separate denomination from Christians who hold the same faith and the same form of government, but who usually baptize by a different method. If they can fellowship as churches in separate denominations, they can fellowship as churches in the same denomination. If Free Baptists and Congregationalists, for example, are not united in one denomination, it is not because they are kept apart by anything essential or anything which they think to be important, but simply because they have not taken the trouble to come together. That they have not taken the trouble is not to their credit.

"Close communion is the only logical position which can be taken by those who believe that all other denominations except themselves disobey a plain, binding command of God. That is the position which close communion Baptists take. They say that the command is to believe and be baptized, and that the two commands are equally binding even if not of equal saving value."

All that I am insisting upon is that the Lord's

Supper is a church ordinance, and that no one can participate in it who is not subject to the discipline of the church. Dr. Hibbard, the great Methodist, frankly says: "On the contrary, the eucharist, from its very nature, is a church ordinance and as such can be properly participated in only by church members. As a church ordinance, it can never be carried out of the church. This is so evident that no words can make it more plain, or add to its force." (Hibbard on Baptism, P. 2, p. 185.)

The Scriptures are plain. All who will not obey the commands of Christ are to be treated as disorderly, and no disorderly person is to be admitted to the Lord's Supper. "Now we command you, brethren, in the name of our Lord Jesus Christ, that ye withdraw yourselves from every brother that walketh disorderly, and not after the tradition received of us. And if any man obey not our word by this epistle, note that man, and have no company with him, that he may be ashamed." (2 Thes. 3:6,14.) And that this is to apply to the Lord's Supper we are plainly told: "But now I have written unto you not to keep company, if any man that is called a brother be a fornicator, or covetous, or an idolater, or a railer, or a drunkard, or an extortioner; with such a one no not to eat." (1 Cor. 5:11.)

If this is not true, church discipline is worse than useless. An open communion church could turn out a member for outrageous wickedness, to-morrow he goes and joins some other denomination, and the next Sunday, when the open communion table is spread, he comes up smiling, and communes with the very church that excluded him. The result of the whole matter is that the church is disgraced; its discipline dishonored and rendered nugatory, and all on account of the unreasonable practice that is called open communion.

I quote again from the *Advance:* "As to the effect of a table open to all, it appears to us to be subversive of church discipline, and to tend in the end to decrease rather than to increase the number of attendants.

"Of what use is it to *excommunicate* a reprobate, by vote of a church, during the week, and then to *communicate* with him if he chooses to come, at one of these open tables, on the next Lord's day! And then the Unitarians and Universalists, practicing on that plan, have found that few wanted what everybody could have. When the boundary line of church and world is thus removed, there is no rush into the church, because church ceases to mean anything. In no denomination is the Lord's table so crowded as where it is made strictly a church ordinance, and no one is invited unless he has openly and permanently professed Christ by uniting with the church."

If the Supper is not under the control of the church, who is responsible for its right administration? Will you say there are, and ought to be, no limits thrown around the Lord's table? Will you say that devils and wicked men ought to sit down to it, and make it a feast of drunken madness instead of Christian joy? If there are qualifications, who is to judge of those qualifications? Manifestly the church of God. By all of these admissions it would necessary follow that in prescribing terms to the Lord's table we have not gone beyond our right. But rather, we have taken the terms prescribed in the word of God, and thrown them around the table as a safeguard. We propose to be liberal, and no more liberal, than was Christ our Lord. You talk much about a common table, why not have a common baptism? If you will obey the commands of the Bible, there will be no strife on this subject.

Hence George T. Ladd says: "But this right of discipline cannot be duly exercised, except upon the principle of a regenerate membership. The wrong in communing in the most holy sacraments acts with these, who, neither in faith nor conduct, claimed the spiritual communion upon which the sacraments take place, could be amended only by an application of the same principle. 'The people are the church,' said Robinson, 'and to make a reformed church there must first be a reformed people.' It is only by the grace of God in their hearts, he goes on to maintain, that the people, 'being first fitted for and made capable of the sacraments and other ordinances, might afterward have communicated in the pure use of them.' Christ believed on and confession is, in judgment of them all, and according to the words of Davenport, 'the rock whereon a particular visible church is built.' It was, therefore, as a fundamental doctrine, almost without a single exception even so much as questioned by our early authorities, that the Cambridge Platform laid down its definitions." (Principles of Church Polity, p. 51.)

And there is no way to purify the church except by discipline.

It is not a matter of liberality, but of church duty, to reject from the table of the Lord those who have never obeyed the requirements of God's word. Dr. Hibbard, and I am delighted to agree so readily with this great Methodist, makes another point so just that I am constrained to quote him again. "If it be a responsible act to reject them," says he, "in the absence of an express interdict; certainly it is not less responsible to admit them in the absence of an express command. If, in rejecting them, there is danger of offending a 'little one that believes' in Christ; so also, in receiving them, there is danger of diverting the ordinance from its intended application, and profaning its sanctity. If express precept is what the advocates of mixed communion demand, certainly they are in no better case than we are. And we have the same authority for rejecting, as they have for receiving unbaptized persons to the table of the Lord; and, as far as we can judge, they incur a responsibility of no less magnitude than we ourselves. The truth is, that THE PREPONDERANCE OF SCRIPTURE EVIDENCE IS AGAINST MIXED COMMUNION." (On Baptism, p. 186.)

CHAPTER XVI.

INFANT COMMUNION.

I HAVE already showed that our terms of communion are as liberal as those of any other denomination of Christians. May I suggest that we are more liberal at the Lord's table than the most of Christian denominations. We do commune with our own membership, the most of other denominations do not. The Methodists do not commune with all of their members. The Presbyterians do not. These denominations have baptized members that are not admitted to their own table. An infant, though it may have been made "federally holy," or "brought by baptism into the Church of Christ," is excluded from a Methodist or Presbyterian communion table. We are at least liberal enough to commune with our own members.

I am not trifling. There is quite as much to prove infant communion as there is to prove infant baptism. They rest upon the same argument; and the traditional history that would prove the antiquity of the one would prove the antiquity of the other. The Greek Church when it baptizes an infant also admits it to the Lord's table and feeds the child with a spoon.

INFANT COMMUNION. 213

I shall introduce some authorities on infant communion.

Bingham says: Nor was this confirmation after baptism "only true with respect to adult persons, but also with respect to infants, who were anciently confirmed with the imposition of hands and the holy chrism, or unction, as soon as they were baptized; which will, perhaps, seem a paradox to many who look no further than the practice of later ages: but it may be undeniably learned in two ways. 1. From the plain testimony of the ancients declaring it to be so; and 2. From that known custom and usage of the church, in giving the eucharist to infants, which ordinarily presupposes their confirmation." (Antiquities Christian Church, B. XII, C. 1, vol. 1, p. 544.)

Salmasius, a learned Catholic, says: "It was the invariable practice to give the catechumens the eucharist immediately after they were baptized. Afterwards the opinion prevailed that no one could be saved unless he were baptized, so the custom of baptizing infants was introduced. And because to adult catechumens, as soon as they were baptized, no space of time intervening, the eucharist was given, so after pedobaptism was introduced, this was also done in the case of infants." (Trans., p. 495.)

Bishop Bossuet affirms: "The church has always believed, and still believes, that infants are capable of receiving the eucharist as well as baptism, and finds no more obstacle to their communion in the words of St. Paul, 'Let a man examine himself and so let him eat;' than she finds to their baptism in these words of the Lord, 'Teach and baptize.' But as she knew that the eucharist could not be absolutely necessary to their salvation, after they had received the full remission of sins in their baptism, she believed it was a matter of discipline to give or not to give the communion in this age; thus it is that during the first eleven or twelve centuries she, for good reasons, gave it; and for other reasons, equally good, has since then ceased to give it." (Traite Com., P. i, p. 3.)

Gieseler says: "The use of exorcism is distinctly mentioned, and all who had been baptized, even the children, partook of the eucharist." (Church History, vol. 1, p. 159.)

Lundy, Episcopalian, says: "All, therefore, whether young or old, whether infants at the breast or those who had attained their full growth and maturity of body and mind, were alike baptized and alike partook of this heavenly manna. Otherwise, they must have perished. Baptism and the Eucharist, therefore, are for infants, just as much as for adults; and the Eucharist was given to infants in the universal church until the Council of Trent abolished the practice. Rather, it was the common use in the two Churches, of the East and the West down to the twelfth century, when the Latin Church began to discontinue the practice, until its official abolishment by the Council of Trent in the sixteenth century. It was the twenty-first session of that Council, the fifth under Pius IV, that decreed an anathema against all who held or taught that both species of bread and wine were necessary to the validity of the Eucharist, coupling with this the anathema against the communion of infants. The first canon of that session is this: 'If any one shall say, from the Word of God that it is necessary to salvation for each or all the faithful of Christ that they ought to receive both species of the most holy sacrament of the Eucharist, let him be accursed.' And then follows canon IV, which is this: 'If any one shall say, that the communion of the eucharist is necessary for children before they come to years of discretion, let him be accursed.'" (Monumental Christianity, p. 376.)

Dr. Coleman, Presbyterian, says: "After the general introduction of infant baptism the sacrament continued to be administered to all who had been baptized, whether infants or adults. The reason alleged by Cyprian and others for this practice was, that age was no impediment. Augustine strongly advocates the practice. The custom continued for several centuries. It is mentioned in the third Council of Tours, A. D.

813; and even the Council of Trent, A. D. 1545, only decreed that it should not be considered essential to salvation. It is still scrupulously observed by the Greek Church." (Ancient Christianity Exemplified, C. 22, sec. 8, p. 310.)

Schaff, Presbyterian, says: In North Africa, "in Cyprian's time, we find the custom of infant communion (administered with wine alone) which was justified from John 6:53, and has continued in the Greek (and Russian) church to this day, though irreconcilable with the apostle's requisition of a preparatory examination." (History Christian Church, vol. 2, p. 239.)

Dr. Bennett, Methodist, says: "Since the church from the beginning of the third century accounted infants as proper subjects of infant baptism, and regarded this as the proper initiatory rite into the Church—ratifying the membership by the holy unction and confirmation—she consistently admitted infants to the Lord's Supper. Of this there is abundant proof as early as the third century." (Archæology, p. 424.)

The fathers make the practice of infant communion well nigh universal. For the East, where it still flourishes, we have the testimony of the so-called liturgy of Clement, in which little children (*paidia*) are ordered to receive immediately after all who have any special dedication, "and then all the people in order." (Constit. Apostles, l. viii, c. 13.) Pseudo-Dyonisius, possibly of the fifth century, but more probably of the sixth, says that "children who cannot understand divine things are yet made partakers of divine generation, and of the divine communion of the most sacred mysteries." (De Eccl. Hierarch., c. vii, sec. 11.) Evagrius, who completed his history in 594, proves the continued observance of the rite, where he mentions an "ancient custom" at Constantinople, "when there remained a good quantity of the holy portions of the undefiled body of Christ our God, uncorrupted boys from among those who attended the school of the undermaster were sent to consume them." (lib. iv, c. 36.) There is a story told by John Moschus, A. D. 630, of some children who imitated among themselves the celebration of the Eucharist, as they had witnessed and taken part in it themselves." (Pratum Spirit., c. 196.)

The earliest witness in the Latin church is Cyprian, who writing in 251, relates how the agitation of an infant to whom the cup was offered, led to the discovery of its having been taken to a heathen sacrifice. He also represents the children of apostates as able to plead at the day of judgment: "We have done nothing; nor have we hastened of our own accord to those profane defilements, forsaking the meat and cup of the Lord." (De Lapsis.) Augustine says: "They are infants; but they are made partakers of his Table, that they may have life in themselves." (Sermon 174, sec. 7.)

The same practice was common in England. Hart says: "Infant communion was a very ancient practice, and is said to have prevailed generally in the church for six hundred years. In the address of our countryman Ælfric to the priesthood at the delivery of the chrism, he says: 'Ye should give the Eucharist to children when they are baptized, and let them be brought to mass that they may receive it all the seven days that they are unwashed.'" (Eccl. Rec., p. 188.) So late as A. D. 1073, infant communion was still practiced in England. (Wilkin's Concilia Magnæ Brit., vol. 1, p. 361.)

It is useless to assert that this is of no importance. Dr. Dwight declares this is a matter of much importance, and that the teaching of the Pedobaptists on this point is erroneous. Says he: "It is objected further that all baptized persons are by that class of Christians to whom I have attached myself, considered as members of the Christian church; yet those who are baptized in infancy, are not treated as possessed of that character; particularly, they are not admitted to the sacramental supper; nor made objects of ecclesiastical discipline. As this object has in my own view, a more serious import than any other which has been alleged, it deserves particular consideration. In the first place, I acknowledge without hesitation, that the conduct of those with whom I am in immediate communion, and so far as I know their opinions also, with regard to this subject, are in a greater or less degree, erroneous and indefensible." (Dwight's Theology, Sermon 157, vol. 4, p. 317.)

From the above reasoning I reach two conclusions: 1. Infant communion is as authoritative as infant baptism. 2. And what is more to our point, as long as our Pedobaptist friends disregard the voice of all antiquity, and will not commune with their own children, they ought not to accuse us of being illiberal. We, at least, do commune with our own membership.

CHAPTER XVII.

OPEN COMMUNIONISTS DO NOT ENDORSE EACH OTHER.

OPEN communionists make a great show of Christian union; and yet they say the most bitter and harsh things against each other. They make a show of endorsing each other when they celebrate together, which is seldom, the Lord's Supper; and the rest of the time they spend in denouncing each other's doctrines. This is neither good sense nor good policy. I shall indicate some points of difference among open communionists.

1. Some one may say that to have an open table is not an endorsement of each other's doctrines. I claim that where one denomination sits down to the Lord's Supper with another denomination it thereby says we have no differences between us. It is an endorsement of the other's position; and it is invariably so understood by the people. It says: "Your church is as good as mine; and really there is no difference between us." If that is the truth, why have two separate organizations? For men to sit down to the Lord's table proclaiming that there is no difference between Christians, and then to get up and perpet-

uate party strife and antagonistic organizations, is sinful in the sight of God. Every reason that would proclaim a common table, would demand a union between such parties. I have no faith in the so-called liberal principles of those who preach unity at an open table, and practice dissensions away from it.

That open communionists understand that joint participation is an endorsement of each other's doctrines is made clear by Dr. Dwight. He says: "In baptism, Christians appear as subjects to this ordinance but once in their lives; and most of them at this appearance, being infants, are altogether passive. At the Lord's Supper they are always voluntary, active partakers; and appear often in this character, throughout their whole Christian life. They appear at the table of Christ in a body; as members of him, the Head. They appear as Christian friends and brethren; and are, all members one of another. They appear as open professors of his religion; as his followers; as attached to his cause; as interested in his death; as expectants of his coming; as voluntary subjects of his government. They exhibit themselves as being united in one Faith, one Baptism, one Worship, one System of Doctrines, and Duties, and one scheme of Communion, and Discipline; as having one common interest, one common pilgrimage, and one final home. All of these things are exhibited and established by the Lord's Supper." (Theology Explained and Defended, vol. 4, p. 364.)

How Methodists, Presbyterians, the "Christian Church," and others can endorse each other's doctrines, as they do at the Lord's table, is beyond my conception. But I shall proceed to point out some differences.

2. They differ in doctrines. Take the Presbyterians and Methodists on the single point of predestination. John Wesley called predestination by every foul name. He says in his sermon on Free Grace, number 54: "This doctrine not only tends to destroy Christian holiness, happiness and good works, but has also a direct and manifest tendency to overthrow the whole Christian revelation. * * * It represents our blessed Lord, as a hypocrite, a deceiver, of the people, a man void of sincerity. * * * It represents the most holy God as worse than the devil; as more false, more cruel, more unjust. * * * This is the blasphemy for which I abhor the doctrine of predestination."

John Calvin was scarcely less bitter in his denunciation of Arminianism. He says: "The enemies of God's predestination are stupid and ignorant and the devil hath plunged out their eyes." "Such men fight against the Holy Ghost, like mad beasts, and endeavor to abolish the holy Scripture. There is more honesty in the

Papists than in these men; for the doctrines of the Papists are a great deal better, more holy, and more agreeable to the sacred Scriptures, than the doctrines of these vile and wicked men, who cast down God's holy election—these dogs that bark at it, and swine that root it up."

Methodists and Presbyterians may not now vilify each other in this way, but they are no nearer agreed on predestination than were Calvin and Wesley.

John Wesley's brother, Charles Wesley, wrote a polemical poem on "The Horrible Decree," in which his poetic genius left him, as may be inferred from the following specimens:

> "Oh horrible Decree,
>   Worthy of whence it came.
> Forgive their hellish blasphemy,
>   Who charge it on the Lamb.
> To limit thee, they dare
>   Blaspheme thee to thy face,
> Deny their fellow worms a share
>   In thy redeeming grace."

In a poem on Predestination, he prays:

> "Increase (if that can be)
>   The perfect hate I feel
> To Satan's Horrible Decree,
>   That genuine child of hell;
> Which feigns thee to pass by
>   The most of Adam's race,
> And leave them in their blood to die,
>   Shut out from saving grace."

Dr. Bledsoe, a great Southern Methodist, is reported to have said: "I would prefer to worship a huge gorilla than the Presbyterian's God."

How a staid, well regulated Presbyterian can sit down to the Methodist Supper and endorse such statements I do not know.

But the Presbyterians have been scarcely less denunciatory of Methodist doctrines. John Calvin said as severe things about Arminianism as John Wesley had about predestination. The Presbyterians have not yet forgiven Wesley. Dr. Schaff sums up Wesley's position thus: "Wesley began to thunder against the imaginary horrors and blasphemies of Calvinism which has since resounded from innumerable Methodist pulpits. He defines predestination to be 'an eternal, unchangeable, irresistible decree of God by virtue of which one part of mankind are infallibly saved, and the rest infallibly damned; it being impossible that any of the former should be damned, and that any of the latter should be saved;' and then he goes on to show that this doctrine makes all preaching useless; that he makes void the ordinances of God; and it tends directly to destroy holiness, meekness, and love. The comfort and happiness of religion, zeal for good works, and the whole Christian religion, that it turns God into a hypocrite and deceiver; that it overturns his justice, mercy and truth, and represents him 'as worse than the devil, more false and more cruel and more unjust.' 'This,' says he, 'is the blasphemy clearly contained in the horrible decree of predestination, and for this I abhor it (however I love the people who assert it.)'" (Creeds of Christendom, vol. 1, pp. 895, 896.)

I submit that people who abuse each other in this manner ought not to talk of the sectarianism of the Baptists.

Perhaps the "Christian Church," or "Disciples," says more about Christian union than any other; and yet the "Disciples" fearfully denounce those who do not agree with them. I present one example out of many that could be chosen. Rev. John F. Rowe, in an article on "Christian Unity," says: "The very fact that the various denominations glory in distinctive titles—in the nomenclature of spiritual Babylon—convinces us of insincerity in seeking Christian union upon the basis of the Bible. While professing to be 'spiritually united,' because they cannot ecclesiastically harmonize, they live in constant fear of each other, and are envious of each other's popularity; and, rather than despise popularity and walk humbly with the humble Christ—walk in the pure light of God's word—they willfully adhere to what they know to be disturbing elements to the peace of the Church. In this state of mind they are neither spiritually nor ecclesiastically united. Whenever all of these parties as individuals shall come to be united in Christ, their spiritual Head (and some think they see the golden day approaching), all of this ecclesiastical trumpery will be relegated to the dark dominions of Babylon, whence it came. Christian unity stands still until this turn is made. It is the love of power—the love of ecclesiastical distinction—and the pride of opinionism, which prevents the consummation of Christian unity." (Christian Review, 1887, p. 233.)

I have been long persuaded that those who are the loudest in their abuse of Baptists and Close Communion, and are disposed to make the most capital out of it, are insincere and make this a rallying cry of strife. Sectarianism and a desire for popularity is at the bottom of the whole open-communion business. Whenever you hear a man, or denomination, boasting how wonderfully liberal he or it is, and that "one church is as good as another," you may know that the whole thing is false, and that he is the most bitter sectarian in the country. What we need at this time is Christian manliness, an open-hearted declaration of what we believe, an honest appeal to the word of God; then the day of Christian union is not far away.

3. In church government. Dr. Charles Hodge so admirably states the case that I gladly adopt his words. He says: "It is clearly impossible that Romanists and Protestants should be united

in the same ecclesiastical organization. It is no less impossible that anything more than a federal union, such as may exist between independent nations, can be formed between Prelatists and Presbyterians, between Baptists and Pedobaptists, between Congregationalists and any other denomination recognizing the authority of Church Courts. The principles conscientiously adopted by these different bodies are not only different, but antagonistic and incompatible. Those who hold them can no more form one church than despotism and democracy can be united in the constitution of the same State. If by divine right all authority vests in the king, it cannot vest in the people. The advocates of these opposite theories therefore cannot unite in one form of government. It is no less obvious that if ecclesiastical power vests in one man—the bishop—it cannot vest in the presbytery. Episcopalians and Presbyterians cannot therefore unite. The latter deny the right of the bishop to the prerogatives which he claims; and the former deny the right of the presbytery which it assumes. The same thing is equally plain of Presbyterians and Congregationalists. The former regard themselves as bound by the decisions of sessions and presbyteries; the latter refuse to recognize the right of Church courts to exercise discipline or government. So long, therefore, so much difference exist among Christians, it is plain that Romanists, Episcopalians, Presbyterians and Congregationalists, must form separate and independent bodies." (Church Polity, p. 96.)

If Dr. Hodge is right in this, and he undoubtedly is, why do Methodists and Presbyterians on "sacramental occasions" go through the solemn mockery of saying: "There is no difference, one church is as good as another." Why then not unite in one organization? If there "is no difference" in keeping up different churches, and thus dividing the Christian world, they are sinning before God. There is a difference, great and mighty barriers have been placed in the way of Christian union. The very thing that would keep them from uniting in one organization would logically keep them from communing together. Quit preaching union that never unites; and show us something of the beautiful fruits of real union.

Not only are these denominations at war with one another, they are not at peace among themselves. The various and sundry branches of Methodists ought to come to some agreement among themselves, before they preach too often on "Baptist close communion." In a number of the States two different Methodist bodies are striving to occupy the same territory. It is no uncommon thing to find in a little village, scarcely able to support one church, two rival Methodist churches; and the vindictive rivalry is not edifying to an outsider. The "Northern and Southern Methodists" are not in heavenly accord. The following clipping from a well-known newspaper does not overstate the case:

"The Southern Methodist church having, through its representatives in the Council, declined for the hundredth time to commit suicide as a church, and turn its effects over to the North, the Northern bishops could no longer restrain the full expression of their brotherly love. In a recent consultation of war, not against the world, the flesh and the devil, but against Southern Methodists, Bishop Fowler said: 'They are as thoroughly rebel as they ever were.' 'That's so,' said Bishop Mallalieu, and added: 'We have gained the cause in Kentucky, Missouri and Tennessee, and driven the Southern Methodists to their dens; and what we have done there we can do in the next belt.' The 'dens' in Louisville are very handsome large buildings, filled with congregations.

"To say the least of it, the Methodist millennium is not yet."

There is at this time, 1892, in progress a violent discussion between the Northern and Southern Methodists. Bishop Merrill, claiming to write in a spirit of conservatism, has written a book on the "Organic Union of American Methodism," that is little less than a smoking volcano.

He says of the Southern Methodists: "It was noticeable that the representatives of the Methodist Episcopal Church, South, remained silent on that occasion (at the Ecumenical Conference) so far as organic union was concerned. From that silence, and from the comments afterward made in their papers, it is readily inferred that those in position to direct public sentiment in the Southern Church are opposed to the agitation of this subject. For years past there has been a studied effort on their part to avoid this discussion." (Organic Union, p. 20.)

And of the tremendous task of uniting these two Methodist factions, he says: "To expect this grand consummation to be brought about without an effort, would be visionary indeed. Time, study, preparation, and sacrifice will be required; and this, after the purpose has been formed to reach the end, as well as in the preliminary steps that lead to that purpose. He who fails to appreciate the magnitude of the undertaking is not prepared for the discussion of the subject, nor to sit in judgment on the issue when it is presented. No thoughtful person will look upon it as other than an enterprise of proportions equal to anything heretofore attempted in the history of religious denominations." (Organic Union, pp. 9, 10.) But the Bishop says he is not sanguine of this result in his day.

Dr. E. E. Hoss, Editor of the Nashville *Chris-*

tian Advocate, ends a lengthy review of Bishop Merrill's book with a challenge for a public written discussion. Among other things, he says: "There is no mistaking Bishop Merrill's object. He avows that it is his desire to promote the consolidation of the various branches of American Methodism into one compact and powerful organization. It is our duty to tell him with the utmost plainness of speech that his book will help to delay the consummation of such a result. Though he sets out with the manifest purpose to be fair and just, he does not go far till he shows that he is largely under the dominion of sectional and ecclesiastical prejudice. His method of approach to our Church is much as if he should say: 'Come, come my good brethren, in all of the disputes between us you have been wholly in the wrong. I call upon you in the most fraternal spirit to abandon your convictions, and to accept mine in their place.' Whether this is the proper temper in which the healing of an old quarrel should be undertaken, we shall not pause to consider." (Christian Advocate, February 18th, 1892.)

The fraternal messenger of the Methodist Episcopal Church, South, sent to the General Conference, at Omaha, was hissed while on the floor of that body. The New Orleans *Christian Advocate*, May 26th, 1892, says:

"The dispatches state that when our fraternal messenger to the General Conference, at Omaha, Dr. J. J. Tigert, in the course of his speech to that body, remarked that the 'Southern whites were the negroes' best friends,' the statement was greeted with hissings! This was an unpardonable offense. The M. E. Church had as well cease prating about fraternity and union, if our representative to their highest body is to be treated with such indignity and no protest made as publicly as the hissing was done!"

I have no disposition to enter into a discussion of this nature, but I do wish to say, that until the Methodists quit perpetrating upon the Christian world, such discussions as these, in all good conscience they ought to cease talking about "Baptist close communion," even though it be as bad as the average Methodist pictures it to be.

The Presbyterians are scarcely better off than the Methodists, with this additional difficulty that their discussions are on the most vital questions of doctrine.

And the Episcopalians come forward and declare that the Presbyterians are not ordained. Palmer says: "These questions, however, are not essential in the discussion of the Presbyterian ordinations; for it is certain, that such ordinations having been performed without any necessity, and in opposition to the authority of the bishops of Scotland, were in their origin *illegitimate* and *schismatical;* and the Catholic church in all ages has rejected such ordinations, and accounted them null; therefore the Presbyterian establishment being founded in schism, and destitute of an apostolic ministry, constitutes no part of the visible church of Christ." (Church of Christ, vol. 1, p. 443.)

We Baptists humbly suggest that our own doctrines are scriptural and rational, and that our Methodist and Presbyterian brethren have ample opportunities to invest their spare time in looking after their own schisms.

4. Open communionists do not agree among themselves as to the nature and design of the Lord's Supper. They will sit down and eat of the bread and drink of the wine, and get up and wrangle over the significance of the thing they have done. One declares that he ate of the body and blood of the Son of God; and the other denies that it is more than a remembrance of the Son of God. The mere observance of the Lord's Supper has never been a bond of union for a moment to a single congregation. The whole thing of open communion is farcical, unscriptural and impolitic.

CHAPTER XIX.

OPEN COMMUNION IS A WORN OUT HERESY BORROWED FROM THE BAPTISTS.

THE fact is that the whole system of open communion originated with the Baptists, and has been borrowed from us by others. Previous to John Bunyan, and some of his followers, open communion was not heard of in the world. Open communion was not found in the Bible, but borrowed from the Baptists. It is an old heresy that we well nigh discarded long ago, because it was not Scriptural nor practical, and in more recent years some people think they have made a great discovery.

Among the Baptists of England open communion has never had more than a transient popularity. Our Confessions of Faith have all, with one exception, and that one does not mention the subject, been in favor of restricted communion. I quote these Confessions, not as authoritative, for Baptists recognize nothing as authoritative except the holy Scriptures, but as giving our position and history in regard to this ordinance. (See Confessions of Faith of the Baptist Churches of England, London, 1854.)

From the Schleitheim Confession, one of the

oldest Baptist documents known, 1527: "All who would break one bread for a memorial of the broken body of Christ, and all who would drink one draught as a memorial of the poured out blood of Christ, should before hand be united to one body of Christ; that is, to the church of God, of which the head is Christ, to-wit, by baptism."

From the Confession of John Smyth and his church, 1610: "The holy Supper, according to the institution of Christ, is to be administered to the baptized; as the Lord Jesus hath commanded that whatsoever he hath appointed should be taught to be observed."

From another and longer form of the same: "That only the baptized are to taste the elements of the Lord's Supper."

From the Confession of Seven London Churches, 1544: "Baptism is an ordinance of the New Testament, given by Christ, to be dispensed upon persons professing faith, or that are made disciples; who, upon profession of faith, ought to be baptized, and after to partake of the Lord's Supper."

From the appendix to the above, prepared by Benjamin Cox: "Though a believer's right to the use of the Lord's Supper do immediately flow from Jesus Christ apprehended and received by faith; yet inasmuch as all things ought to be done not only decently, but also in order, 1 Cor. 14:40; and the Word holds forth this order, that disciples should be baptized, Matt. 28:19; Acts 2:38; and then be taught to observe all things (that is to say, all other things) that Christ commanded the Apostles, Matt. 28:20; and accordingly the Apostles first baptized disciples, and then admitted them to the use of the Supper, Acts 2:4-42; we therefore do not admit any to the use of the Supper, nor communicate with any in the use of this ordinance, but disciples baptized, lest we should have fellowship with them in their doing contrary to order."

From the Somerset Confession, 1656: "That it is the duty of every man and woman, that have repented from the dead works, and have faith toward God, to be baptized * * * And being thus planted in the visible church or body of Christ * * * do walk together in communion, in all the commandments of Jesus. * * * That we believe some of those commandments further to be as followeth: 1. Constancy in prayer. 2. Breaking of bread," etc. (The omissions are mainly passages of Scripture quoted in proof of the statements.)

From a brief Confession of Faith (London, 1660): "That the right and only way of gathering churches (according to Christ's appointment, Matt. 28:19,20) is first to teach or preach the gospel (Mark 16:16) to the sons and daughters of men; and then to baptize (that is English, to dip) in the name of the Father, Son, and Holy

Spirit, or in the name of the Lord Jesus Christ, such only of them as profess repentance towards God, and faith toward our Lord Jesus Christ. * * * That is the duty of such who are constituted as aforesaid, to continue steadfastly in Christ's and the Apostles' doctrines, and assembling together, in fellowship, in breaking of bread, and prayers (Acts 2:42)."

From an Orthodox Creed, 1678: "And no unbaptized, unbelieving, or open profane, or wicked heretical persons, ought to be admitted to this ordinance to profane it."

The only Baptist Confession extant that fails to speak explicitly for restricted communion is that of 1698, which is designedly silent for the reason stated in the appendix to that document: "We are not insensible, that as to the order of God's house, and entire communion therein, there are some things wherein we (as well as others) are not at full accord among ourselves; as for instance, the known principle and state of the consciences of divers of us, that have agreed in this confession is such, that we cannot hold church communion with any other than baptized believers, and churches constituted of such; yet some others of us have a greater liberty and freedom in our spirits that way; and, therefore, we have purposely omitted the mention of things of that nature, that we might concur in giving this evidence of our agreement, both among ourselves and with other good Christians, in those important articles of the Christian religion, mainly insisted on by us; and this, notwithstanding, we all esteem it our chief concern, both among ourselves and all others that in every place call upon the name of the Lord Jesus Christ our Lord, both theirs and ours, and love him in sincerity, to endeavor to keep the unity of the spirit in the bond of peace; and in order thereunto, to exercise all lowliness and meekness, with long-suffering, forbearing one another in love."

After Bunyan's time the controversy dropped until the latter part of the eighteenth century. Baptists, and so far as I know no one else, held to open communion.

Abraham Booth, in his able Vindication of the Baptists, gives the exact history of this thing. He says: "If we appeal to the persuasion and practice of Christians in all ages and nations, it will clearly appear, that baptism was universally considered, by the churches of Christ, as a divinely appointed prerequisite to the Lord's Supper, till about the middle of the last (eighteenth) century, here in England, when some few of the Baptists began to call it in question, and practically to deny it. This our brethren now do who defend and practice free communion. * * * The ingenious author of the 'Pilgrim's Progress' was one of the first in this Kingdom who dared to assert that the want of baptism is 'no bar to communion,' and acted accordingly." (Booth's Apology for the Baptists, Works, vol. 2, pp. 360, 361, 364.)

Dr. Wall says the Baptists of his time were strict communionists. "I know," says he, "that the antipædobaptists do not admit to the Lord's Supper, when it is administered by themselves, any but that are baptized in their way. * * * One thing I am persuaded of concerning the antipædobaptists; and that is, that if they were convinced that this joining in the public service of the Church were lawful and practicable for them, they would join at another rate than some shifting people do nowadays. I take them generally to be cordial, open, and frank expressers of their sentiments." (Wall's History Infant Baptism, vol. 1, pp. 686, 688.)

That open communion originated with the Baptists, and was an unheard-of thing, is amply proved by Dr. John Dick, the eminent Presbyterian scholar. Dr. Dick says: "Our Lord has shown for whose use this ordinance is intended, by administering it to his disciples; and a conclusion may be deduced from the passover, to which the Israelites alone had access, and those who had joined themselves to them by submitting to circumcision. 'This is the ordinance of the passover: There shall no stranger eat thereof. And when a stranger shall sojourn with thee, and will keep the passover of the Lord, let all his males be circumcised, and then let him come near and keep it, and he shall be as one that is born in the land: for no uncircumcised person shall eat thereof.' Since circumcision was an indispensable qualification for eating the passover, it follows that baptism, which has succeeded to it, is requisite to entitle a person to a seat to the table of the Lord. I do not know that this was ever called in question till lately, that a controversy has arisen among the English Baptists, whether persons of other Christian denominations may not be occasionally admitted to the holy communion with them; and it became necessary for those who adopted the affirmative, to maintain that baptism is not a previous condition. This assertion arose out of the peculiar system, which denies the validity of infant baptism. But to every man who contents himself with a plain view of the subject, and has no purpose to serve by subtleties and refinements, it will appear that baptism is as much the initiating ordinance of the Christian, as circumcision was of the Jewish dispensation. An uncircumcised man was not permitted to eat the passover, and an unbaptized man should not be permitted to partake of the Eucharist." (Dick's Theology, Lecture 92, p. 421.)

It was the eloquent Robert Hall that made open communion popular. In common with all other Baptists he rejected infant baptism and affusion. He did not believe that Pedobaptists were baptized at all. He likewise held that baptism was not a prerequisite to communion.

Pastor Charles H. Spurgeon is often quoted in this connection. His view was somewhat peculiar. In speaking of a visit to Mr. Spurgeon, in May, 1881, Rev. H. L. Wayland, D.D., editor of the *National Baptist*, writes in that paper, July 7th, 1881, as follows: "Having heard varying statements as to his views of the communion question, I thought I would not lose the opportunity of learning at first hands what his position was. He said: 'We occupy a conservative position among our churches on that matter. I believe that baptism and the Lord's Supper are the privilege of all Christians. I believe that any Christian has a right to be baptized; and any Christian has a right to baptize, and especially any minister. So I believe any Christian has a right to partake of the Lord's Supper. When I am at Mentone, it is a great pleasure to me to break bread for all Christians who desire to unite in the Supper. But I do not believe that any one should be admitted to the church without baptism. If any person of credible Christian character comes to us and asks to be admitted to the Lord's Supper, we give him the privilege for three months, at the end of that time we say to him: 'You have had an opportunity to know our views and our practice; if you choose to unite with us, we shall be glad to receive you. If not, you had better go to those with whom you are in fuller sympathy.' And in ninety-nine times out of an hundred the person says: 'I have seen your ways; and I am satisfied to be baptized.'"

No man denounced infant baptism, and especially infant baptismal salvation, with more terrific severity than did Mr. Spurgeon. Yet he practically nullified this by allowing the unbaptized to commune with his church; but he did not permit them to become members until they had been immersed upon a profession of their faith. At the end of three months, if such persons did not wish to be baptized, they were asked to discontinue their approach to the communion table. Their non-membership, said Mr. Spurgeon, rendered them ineligible to church membership; their non-baptism, say I, rendered them ineligible to the Lord's Supper. I go farther than this, and say, that membership in a Scriptural church is a supreme prerequisite to the Lord's Supper, while baptism is a prerequisite because it is indispensable to church membership. All that is needed to refute the opinion of Robert Hall and Mr. Spurgeon is the commission of our Lord: "Go disciple all nations, baptizing them," etc. It is perfectly evident that discipleship preceded baptism, and between discipleship and baptism, which is an immediate duty upon believing, there is no room for the observance of the Lord's Supper.

I am sure that Spurgeon was not antagonistic to Baptist principles, as held by us in America. Dr. William E. Hatcher writes, in the *Religious Herald*, March 3rd, 1892: "But it yet remains to record his most emphatic and memorable utterance with reference to the American Baptists: 'I have,' he said, 'not one word of unfriendly criticism to utter against my Baptist brethren beyond the Atlantic. On the contrary, I believe that the Baptists of America are the best Baptists in the world, and that the best Baptists in America are the Baptists of the South. Moreover, if I were to come to America to live, I would join a close communion church and conform myself to its practices on the Communion question.' As we talked further, he said that it was impossible for an outsider fully to understand the Baptist situation in England, and even the little that I saw and heard convinced me that American Baptists need to exercise charity and forbearance toward their English brethren. They have persecutions and complications to which we are strangers, and if they do not hold all of the distinctive views for which we stand, we ought, at least, to rejoice for such testimony, in favor of the truth, as they are so nobly bearing."

The *Journal and Messenger* publishes a paper on Spurgeon, read before the Cleveland Baptist Ministers' Conference, by the Rev. W. A. Perrins, late of Spurgeon's College, which gives valuable testimony concerning the great preacher's views on "close communion."

Mr. Perrins says: "Wrong impressions have gone abroad in regard to his position in respect to the communion question. This has led some other denominations to claim him as their own. But he was a Baptist to the backbone and at heart a close communionist. My last interview with him, a few days previous to my leaving for this country, proves this. After a very lengthy conversation on subjects relative to American theology, he said: 'Have you made up your mind on the communion question? You are going to a country where the majority of Baptists are close communionists. Really, if I had to begin my ministry again, I should certainly commence with a close-communion church. I am led to believe the American Baptists are right, but I cannot alter the usages of my church, which have been of so long standing.'"

Dr. Edward Parker, President of the Manchester Baptist College, when in America in 1889, said that Mr. Spurgeon was hardly looked upon in England as an Open Communionist, and Mr. Spurgeon said of himself: "As compared with the bulk of English Baptists, I am a strict communionist myself, as my church fellowship is strictly of the baptized."

Here then is the origin of open communion. John Bunyan was its father, and Robert Hall its most eloquent advocate. Whenever you hear other denominations boasting of their open communion, a quiet reminder would not be out of place, that open communion is a Baptist heresy, rejected by the most of Baptists, and that it was born over sixteen hundred years this side of the apostles.

But up to this time open communion has not prevailed among the Baptists of Great Britain, nor is it likely to prevail. The open communion wing is rapidly declining, while the restricted communionists are constantly gaining ground. Rev. D. O. Davis, of Rockdale, England, addressed the Southern Baptist Convention, in May, 1891. Among other things he said was that the close communionists constituted a majority of the Baptists of Great Britain. His figures were as follows: "In Wales there are ninety thousand four hundred and seventy-nine Baptists, almost to a man close communionists. In Scotland, thirty-three thousand six hundred and thirty-seven, nearly all close communionists, so that we have in Wales and Scotland one hundred and twenty-five thousand one hundred and sixteen close communionists. We have in England at least sixty thousand close communionists. In the United Kingdom we have a total of one hundred and eighty-five thousand one hundred and sixteen close communionists. There are one hundred and thirty-four thousand six hundred and thirty-nine open communionists."

THE END.

INDEX OF AUTHORS AND SUBJECTS.

Advance, The...112, 204, 208
Alexander, Dr. Archibald 25
Alford, Henry 36
American Christian Review 162
American Presbyterian .. 84
Antioch, Council of 39
Apostolic Constitutions, 42, 45
Apostolic Times 158, 161
Armitage, Thomas 194
Asbury, Bishop 129, 131, 138–140
Assembly, General 89
Augustine 41, 44, 49, 217

Baird, Robert 17
Bancroft, George 12
Bannerman 55
Baptism 163
Baptismal salvation, 173; taught by The Disciples, 181; Episcopalians, 173; Presbyterians, 175; Methodists.. 177
Baptists, Bigoted, 8; Bible Societies, 20; Charity, 190; Colleges, 16; Confessions of Faith, 234; misunderstood, 7; ignorance of, 15; missions, 19; Newspapers, 17; Persecuted, 74–80, 92–101, 114–117; Religious liberty, 12–15; writers 17
Barnes, Albert 26
Basil 42
Baumgarten 31
Bede, Venerable 43
Beecher, Edward 165
Beecher, Henry Ward.. 111
Belgic Confession..... 62
Bengel 31
Bennett, Dr. C. W..119, 172, 216
Bingham............65, 213
Bledsoe, A. T. .171, 178, 224
Bloomfield............. 34
Blount, J. J............ 31
Bonaventure 43
Booth, Abraham....... 238
Bossuet, Bishop....... 213
Bowman, Bishop...... 146
Breckinridge, Robert.. 101
Broadus, J. A.......... 191
Brownwell, Dr......... 71
Bullinger 82
Bullock, M. G......... 148
Bunsen, Baron........ 40
Bunyan, John...17, 234, 238, 245
Burgess, O. A......... 183

248 INDEX.

Burial of the Dead 72
Burkitt, Wm. 26, 31, 34
Burnet, Bishop 76

Calvin, John.. 28, 31, 81, 92, 98, 176, 222, 224
Campbell, Alexander... 156–158, 181–183
Catholics............... 61
Carthage, Council of. 40, 44
Cary 67
Cassia 45
Catechism, Longer . 90, 185
Caulkins, Dr. W........ 113
Cave................... 66
Chalmers, Thomas 15
Cheetham, S......... 46, 64
Christian Advocate, Nashville 198, 230
Christian Advocate, New York........ 149, 153, 154
Christian Advocate, New Orleans 231
Christian Antiquities, writers on............ 58
Christian Church not in agreement with Pedobaptists, ... 225
Christian Quarterly...... 158
Christian union...... 10, 225
Church of England, Thirty-nine Articles of 62, 66
Church responsibility for discipline......... 202
Church, writers on..... 54
Clarke, Adam... 26, 118, 204
Clement. 41, 216

Close Communion, 7, 21; Christian Church, 156–162; Congregational Church, 109; Episcopal Church, 64; Methodist Church, 118; Presbyterian. 81
Coke, Dr. Thomas,.. 129–139
Coleman, Lyman. 45, 59, 215
Collier 77, 78
Conference, First Methodist 127
Confirmation........... 68
Congregationalist, The... 110
Constitutions and Canons 72
Coronation Oath........ 93
Cox, Benj.............. 235
Cox, Homersham....... 52
Creeds, Confessions, etc. Testimony of 61–63
Curtis................. 192
Cuyler, T. L........ 18, 83
Cyprian 216, 217
Cyril of Jerusalem...... 41

Dabney, Dr............. 57
Davis, D. O............ 245
Dexter, H. M.......... 109
Dick, John.......... 84, 239
Didache, The........... 41
Difference between church communion and Christian communion 190
Discipline, Methodist 63, 118, 141–146, 177
Döllinger........... 42, 47
Drew .. 130, 135, 136, 137, 138
Dudley, Bishop T. U.... 73

INDEX.

	PAGE		PAGE
Dutch Confession	96	Harnack, Dr.	173
Dwight, Dr. T.	109, 218, 221	Hart	218
		Hase	18
Ellicott, C. J.	35	Hatcher, Wm.	243
Engles, Dr.	102	Hawks	80, 100, 131, 138
Episcopal Church, Terms of Communion in the.	64	Hedding, Bishop	141
		Heidelberg Catechism.	62
Episcopalians and Presbyterians not in harmony	232	Helvitic Confession, first, 61, 94; second	62, 94
Errett, I.	159, 183	Hendrix, Bishop	147
Evagrius	217	Henning	79
Evil Livers	71	Herndon, E. W.	160, 184
		Hess	79
Fathers, testimony of	39–49	Hibbard, Dr.	29, 118, 149, 150, 204, 210
Featley, D.	78		
Fisher, George P.	53, 94, 109, 115, 116	Hippolytus	40
		Historical writers	50
Foot	98	Hoadley, Bishop	198
French Confession	96	Hodge, A. A.	91, 186
Froude	75	Hodge, Charles	34, 36, 177, 186, 195, 225
Fuller, Thomas	76, 164		
		Hornbekius	60
Gardner, W. W.	192	Hoss, E. E.	230
Gervinus	13	Hovey, A.	191
Gieseler	51, 214	Hunter, John	87
Gibbon	52		
Gloag	26, 32	Immersion	164
Godet	35	Infant baptism	168
Graham, Robert	158	*Independent, The*	110, 111, 205
Greek Church	44, 61		
Green	60, 86	Infant communion	212
Griffin, Dr.	87	*Interior, The*	21, 86
Gregory and Ruter	53	Irish Articles of Faith.	63
Guericke	48, 59		
Guthrie	100, 176	Jackson	127
		Jacob	55
Hall, John	88	Jefferson, Thomas	97, 98
Hall, Robert	24, 156, 240, 242	Jerome	41
		Jobius	42

INDEX.

	PAGE		PAGE
John's baptism	24	McTyeire, Bishop..121, 124, 126, 128	
Jones, S. P.	187		
Journal and Messenger	244	Mell, P. H.	193
		Melvill	200
Kaye, Bishop	55	Membership, converted.	185
Keener, Bishop	148	Merrill, Bishop	229, 231
Killin, Dr.	55	Methodists not in harmony among themselves, 228; Close communionists, 118–155; Without sacraments for seven years	140
King, P.	47, 65		
Knapp, George	24, 27, 163		
Kurtz	48, 51		
Ladd	209		
Latitudinarianism	8	Meyer	35, 172, 202
Lard, Moses	159, 183	Milman	52
Latimer, Bishop	79	Miscellaneous writers	59
Lecky	169	Montfort, David	107
Lerida, Council of	45	Moschus, J.	217
Liddell and Scott	166, 202	Mosheim	50
Litton	54		
London, Bishop of	133	Neander	48, 50
Lowth, Bishop, asked to ordain a Methodist	128	Nevin	176
Luther	60		
Lundy	214	*Observer, The*	86
		Old Catholic Church	61
Macaulay	17, 175	Olshausen	34, 35
Macknight	34	Oosterzee	34
Madison, President	99	Open communion borrowed from the Baptists, 234; destroys Gospel discipline, 202; open communionists do not endorse each other	220
Malice	71		
Manton, Dr.	60		
Marckius	57		
Martensen, Bishop	58		
Martyr, Justin	39		
Mass, The	44–46	Ordination, Episcopal	66
Mastricht	56	Orthodox Creed	237
Mather, Increase	115	Origin	41, 172
Mathews, R. T.	184		
McDowell	57	Palmer, B. M.	84
McGarvey, J. W.	161	Palmer	232

	PAGE		PAGE
Pan-Presbyterian Council	101	Schaff, Philip.	12, 42, 44, 45, 48, 54, 84, 176, 216, 224
Parker, E.	244	Schismatics	68
Pendleton, J. M.	191	Schleitheim Confession.	234
Perrins	241	Scholars, testimony of.	50–60
Pictetus	56	Scotch Confession	62
Positive and moral law.	197	Scriptural statement	21–38
Prayer Book	69–72, 174	Seven London Churches, Confession of	235
Prerequisites to the Lord's Supper	23, 81	Skeats	12, 120, 124, 126
Predestination	223	Smith, J. Pye	166
Presbyterians and Methodists not agreed in doctrine, 103, 222; Confession of Faith, 81, 85, 88–90, 175, 185; internal troubles of, 229; origin of	92	Smyth, John, Confession of	235
		Sniveley	69
		Somerset, Confession of.	236
		Southey, Robert	123
		Spanheim	51
Pressensè	51, 167	Spurgeon, Charles H., 241–245; not an open communionist	241
Pseudo-Dyonisius	216		
		Stanley, A. P.	36
Quincey	16	Stevens, A.	128, 130
		Steir, Rudolf	60
Ravennellius	59	Stillingfleet, Bishop	47
Recorder, Episcopal	64	Stow	74
Religious Herald	243	Summers, Thomas	188
Resolutions of Southern Baptist Convention.	10, 11	Syriac Version	31, 32
		Systematic Theology and Dogmatics, writers on	56
Riddle	58		
Rives	98		
Roberts, W. C.	82	Tertullian	43, 163
Robertson, J. G.	52	Thayer, J. H.	166, 202
Rules for translating King James' Bible	164	Theophylact	43
		Thompson, Hugh Miller	73
Rushwood	89	Trent, Council of	61
		Turretin	9, 27, 56, 92
Salmatius	213	Tyerman	121, 122, 123, 129, 130, 132, 133, 135, 179
Saxony, Confession of	95		

INDEX.

	PAGE
Valentina, Council of	45
Waddington	52
Wake	69
Wall 49, 65, 76, 175, 239	
Washington, George	14
Watson, Richard	151
Wayland, H. L.	241
Webster	8
Wesley, Charles....122, 125–127, 223	
Wesley, John.........9, 120–125, 131, 179, 222, 223	
Westminster Confession	63
Wheatley	68–70
White, Bishop, Dr. Coke appeals to him for ordination	132
Whitehead	130, 131
Wilkinson, W. C.	195
Williams	69
Williams, Roger	13
Withrow, J. H.......19, 21–23, 114	
Witsius	57
Woods, Dr.	18
Wright, G. W.	111
Zanchius	59

A Biographical Sketch of John Tyler Christian (1854-1925)

BY

JOHN FRANKLIN JONES

A BIOGRAPHICAL SKETCH OF JOHN TYLER CHRISTIAN (1854-1925)

John Tyler Christian—pastor, professor, and historian—was born at Lexington, Kentucky December 14, 1854. The son of Marion Washington and Amanda Martinie Christian, he received both the B.A. and M.A. degrees at Bethel College, Russellville, Kentucky. He traveled to Europe seven times to do postgraduate work.

Christian was ordained in 1876. He held pastorates at First Baptist Church, Chattanooga, Tennessee (1883-86); East Baptist, Louisville, Kentucky (1893-1900); Second Baptist Church, Little Rock, Arkansas (1904-11); First Baptist Church, Hattiesburg, Mississippi (1913-19), et al. He served as Secretary of Missions in Mississippi and later in Arkansas.

He was chairman of an informal conference of friends in Houston, Texas, who met in 1915 to consider founding a theological seminary at New Orleans, Louisiana. Later, he served as chairman of a special committee to bring a recommendation concerning that institution to the Southern Baptist Convention in 1917.

Christian served as professor of Christian History and librarian at Baptist Bible Institute, New Orleans (1919-25) and traveled repeatedly in Europe and the Near East studying and collecting books. He donated his personal library of over 15,000 volumes to Baptist Bible Institute. He was a member of the Society of Christian Archaeology of Greece, the Academy of History of France, the Academy of Science, Arts and Belles Lettres of the Mediterranean, and the American Society of History.

He authored *Close Communion* (1892); *Americanism, or Romanism, Which?* (1895); *Did They Dip? An Examination of the English Baptists* (1897); *Baptist History Vindicated* (1899); *Baptism in Sculpture and Art* (1907); *A History of the Baptists* (1923); and *History of the Baptists of Louisiana* (1923). Christian died December 18, 1925, at New Orleans, Louisiana.

BIBLIOGRAPHY

Encyclopedia of Southern Baptists (1958 ed.). S.v. "Christian, John Tyler," by J. Wash Watts.

BY JOHN FRANKLIN JONES
CORDOVA, TENNESSEE
JULY 2004

THE BAPTIST STANDARD BEARER, INC.

a non-profit, tax-exempt corporation
committed to the Publication & Preservation
of the Baptist Heritage.

CURRENT TITLES AVAILABLE IN
THE BAPTIST *DISTINCTIVES* SERIES

KIFFIN, WILLIAM — A Sober Discourse of Right to Church-Communion. Wherein is proved by Scripture, the Example of the Primitive Times, and the Practice of All that have Professed the Christian Religion: That no Unbaptized person may be Regularly admitted to the Lord's Supper. (London: George Larkin, 1681).

KINGHORN, JOSEPH — Baptism, A Term of Communion. (Norwich: Bacon, Kinnebrook, and Co., 1816)

KINGHORN, JOSEPH — A Defense of "Baptism, A Term of Communion". In Answer To Robert Hall's Reply. (Norwich: Wilkin and Youngman, 1820).

GILL, JOHN — Gospel Baptism. A Collection of Sermons, Tracts, etc., on Scriptural Authority, the Nature of the New Testament Church and the Ordinance of Baptism by John Gill. (Paris, AR: The Baptist Standard Bearer, Inc., 2006).

CARSON, ALEXANDER	Ecclesiastical Polity of the New Testament. (Dublin: William Carson, 1856).
BOOTH, ABRAHAM	A Defense of the Baptists. A Declaration and Vindication of Three Historically Distinctive Baptist Principles. Compiled and Set Forth in the Republication of Three Books. Revised edition. (Paris, AR: The Baptist Standard Bearer, Inc., 2006).
BOOTH, ABRAHAM	Paedobaptism Examined on the Principles, Concessions, and Reasonings of the Most Learned Paedobaptists. With Replies to the Arguments and Objections of Dr. Williams and Mr. Peter Edwards. 3 volumes. (London: Ebenezer Palmer, 1829).
CARROLL, B. H.	*Ecclesia* - The Church. With an Appendix. (Louisville: Baptist Book Concern, 1903).
CHRISTIAN, JOHN T.	Immersion, The Act of Christian Baptism. (Louisville: Baptist Book Concern, 1891).
FROST, J. M.	Pedobaptism: Is It From Heaven Or Of Men? (Philadelphia: American Baptist Publication Society, 1875).
FULLER, RICHARD	Baptism, and the Terms of Communion; An Argument. (Charleston, SC: Southern Baptist Publication Society, 1854).
GRAVES, J. R.	Tri-Lemma: or, Death By Three Horns. The Presbyterian General Assembly Not Able To Decide This Question: "Is Baptism In The Romish Church Valid?" 1st Edition.

	(Nashville: Southwestern Publishing House, 1861).
MELL, P.H.	Baptism In Its Mode and Subjects. (Charleston, SC: Southern Baptist Publications Society, 1853).
JETER, JEREMIAH B.	Baptist Principles Reset. Consisting of Articles on Distinctive Baptist Principles by Various Authors. With an Appendix. (Richmond: The Religious Herald Co., 1902).
PENDLETON, J.M.	Distinctive Principles of Baptists. (Philadelphia: American Baptist Publication Society, 1882).
THOMAS, JESSE B.	The Church and the Kingdom. A New Testament Study. (Louisville: Baptist Book Concern, 1914).
WALLER, JOHN L.	Open Communion Shown to be Unscriptural & Deleterious. With an introductory essay by Dr. D. R. Campbell and an Appendix. (Louisville: Baptist Book Concern, 1859).

For a complete list of current authors/titles, visit our internet site at:
www.standardbearer.org
or write us at:

The Baptist Standard Bearer, Inc.
NUMBER ONE IRON OAKS DRIVE • PARIS, ARKANSAS 72855
TEL # 479-963-3831   FAX # 479-963-8083
EMAIL: Baptist@centurytel.net   http://www.standardbearer.org

Thou hast given a standard to them that fear thee; that it may be displayed because of the truth. — Psalm 60:4

www.ingramcontent.com/pod-product-compliance
Lightning Source LLC
Chambersburg PA
CBHW021806220426
43662CB00006B/199